The Great
MEAT
BALLS
Book

The Great MEAT BALLS Book

JENNIFER BOUDINOT

CHARTWELL
BOOKS

Thank you to everyone who shared recipes, including Michelle Faulkner, Joanne Robinson, and David Boudinot.

This edition published in 2015 by
Chartwell Books
an imprint of Book Sales
a division of Quarto Publishing Group USA Inc.
142 West 36th Street, 4th Floor
New York, New York 10018
USA

ISBN 978-0-7858-3231-7

Packaged by Green Tiger, LLC
Design by S. E. Livingston

Photo Credits: Cover: ©iStock.com/mj0007. Back cover: ©iStock.com/ irakite. 1: ©istockphoto.com/jeniphoto. 7, 23, 51, 79: S.E. Livingston. 8, 64, 66: ©iStock.com/nata_vkusidey. 11: ©iStock.com/Camrocker. 12: ©iStock.comcom/peredniankina.13, 99: ©iStock.com/YelenaYemchuk. 14 (top): ©iStock.com/Ivenks.14 (bottom): ©iStock.com/oleksajewicz. 15: ©Can Stock Photo Inc./markskalny. 16, 114: ©iStock.com/VankaD. 18: ©iStock.com/Elenathewise. 19 (top): ©iStock.com/VibeImages. 19 (bottom): ©iStock.com/angelsimon. 10: ©Can Stock Photo Inc./luknaja. 25: ©iStock.com/travellinglight. 26: ©iStock.com/coloroftime. 28: ©iStock.com/LauriPatterson. 31: ©iStock.com/robynmac. 32: ©iStock. com/Rixipix. 35: ©iStock.com/thisboy. 36: ©iStock.com/neiljlangan. 38: ©iStock.com/og-vision. 40: ©iStock.com/AntonioMP. 42, 47, 113: ©iStock. com/Maria_Lapina. 44: ©iStock.com/msheldrake. 49: ©iStock.com/ penguenstok. 53, 59: ©iStock.com/-Ivinst-. 54: ©iStock.com/MeganBetz. 57: ©iStock.com/annata78. 60: ©iStock.com/shomova. 63: ©iStock. com/Teleginatania. 68: ©123rf.com/Brent HOfacker. 71: ©iStock.com/ fotogal. 73: ©DinnerwithJulie.com (used with permission). 74: ©iStock. com/KellyWendtPhoto. 76: ©iStock.com/DPimborough. 81, 93, 118, 160: ©iStock.com/OlgaMiltsova. 82: ©iStock.com/rez-art. 85: ©iStock.com/ annata. 87: ©iStock.com/Mariha-kitchen. 88: ©iStock.com/mythja. 91: ©iStock.com/bhofack2. 94, 104, 107: ©iStock.com/papkin. 97: ©iStock. com/SMarina. 100: ©iStock.com/tycoon751. 103: ©iStock.com/Taiftin. 109: ©iStock.com/larik_malasha. 110: ©Sally Humeniuk, GoodDinnerMom. com (used with permission). 117, 129, 147: ©iStock.com/Wiktory. 121: ©iStock.com/Fotoscientifica. 123: S.E. Livingston/VectorTemplates.com. 125: ©iStock.com/olgakr. 126: ©iStock.com/Seqoya. 130, 134: ©iStock.com/ Paul_Brighton. 133: ©iStock.com/Beboki. 137: ©iStock.com/Amawasri. 138: ©iStock.com/c_yung. 141, 143: ©iStock.com/vikif. 144: ©iStock.com/ WJBurgwal. 148: ©iStock.com/shtukicrew. 151: ©iStock.com/razmarinka

Printed in China
2 4 6 8 10 9 7 5 3 1

CONTENTS

●●●

Introduction

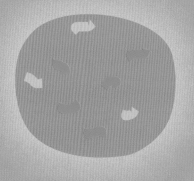

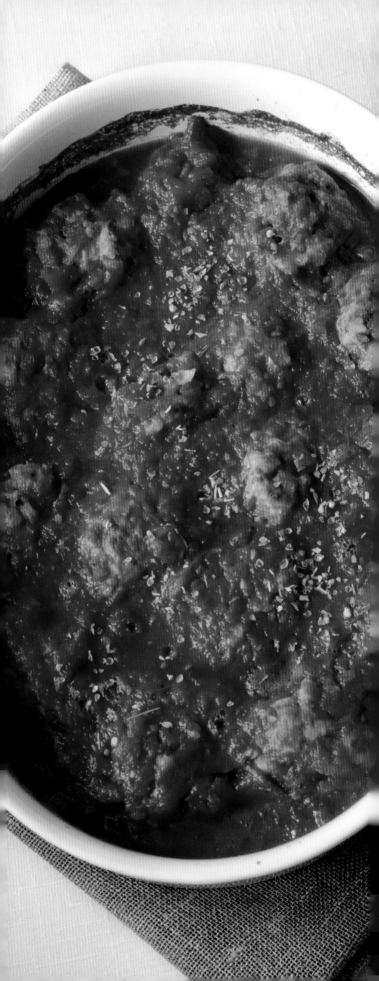

Time for Meatballs!

Everybody loves a meatball. Go ahead—try making one of the many meatballs in this book and putting it in front of your child, a loved one, or even yourself, and see if it doesn't get a smile.

Maybe it's because we like things simple: a sphere, geometrically perfect, but culinarily perfect too: no bones, silverware optional, and easy to pop into your mouth in a couple of bites or less. Meatballs are great as finger-food appetizers, hearty additions to soups, scene-stealing sandwich fillings, and a vast variety of main dishes (all of which you'll find here). They can be easy dinners that your kids will actually eat, but you can also stretch your culinary skills by experimenting with different meats and spices.

Meatballs are so popular that just about every nationality has its own version. You'll find many of them in this book, from Mexican Albóndigas Soup to Russian Katleti Meatballs to Lamb Meatballs from Morocco, along with plenty of variations on the classic Italian-American meatballs we all know and love.

Your Own House Recipe

The meatball recipes in this book not only represent a wide variety of cuisines, but lots of different methods of preparation, including baking, frying, grilling, even cooking in a slow cooker (check out the Easy Slow Cooker Spaghetti and Meatballs on page 83). They comprise all different types of meats (even a couple of vegetarian options like the Vegetarian Rice Balls on page 44 and Falafel Sandwiches on page 77), and contain just about every spice you can think of (see the index on page 156 for a full listing). Follow the recipes as is, or mix and match them to write your own house recipe (space is provided on pages 152-153). Suggestions are included throughout for alternate preparations and sauces, but make sure to use your imagination. The sky's the limit when it comes to meatball ingredients, but don't be surprised if you find yourself falling into something more comfortable. You may end up with a meatball recipe that seems like second nature, and that your family and friends ask for again and again. The recipes in this book will give you a lot of ideas for your own personal meatball creations, but here is some helpful advice for crafting meatballs of any kind.

WHAT'S THE BEST KIND OF MEAT FOR A MEATBALL?

When thinking about meatballs, ground beef might be the first thing to come to mind, but meatballs can be made from any ground meat, poultry, or fish. Meatballs will work best if you use a meat that has about 15-20 percent fat, but they are forgiving—if you use a high-fat grind they might shrink a little more, but they'll still be delicious. Using a leaner meat will make it a bit harder for meatballs to keep their shape during cooking, but you can make up for it by adding plenty of binders like egg and breadcrumbs.

If you have a food processor, you can even grind your own meat—a method preferred by meatball connoisseurs because of the superior texture of coarsely ground meat. Just cut the meat into 2-inch pieces, then lay it flat in a resealable plastic bag in the freezer for an hour. (Partially freezing the meat will make it easier for the blade to slice through it.) Then add it to your food processor fitted with a metal chopping blade in batches and pulse in 2-second bursts 10-15 times.

When grinding your own meat in the food processor, pick a cut with plenty of lines of fat—for beef, chuck and flank steak should work well, but round or "stew meat" is usually too lean. For poultry, use as much dark meat as possible, and mix it with another meat or add some finely chopped skin to make sure it has enough fat. For pork, use butt, and for lamb, shank works best.

Of course, you don't have to go the full-on gourmet, do-it-yourself route for great meatballs. Like any dish, the higher the quality of the meat you use, the tastier your meatballs will be. But the versatility of meatballs means that you can use whatever meat is available or on sale and they'll still taste delicious! Here's what you need to know about store-bought ground meats.

Beef. For a traditional-tasting meatball, use this book's go-to: ground beef. Ground round, which is 85-90 percent lean, is perfect for making meatballs. If making meatballs that contain only beef, stay away from sirloin, which is too lean (higher than 90 percent lean). If ground round isn't available, select chuck, which is 80-85 percent lean.

Veal. If you find ground veal at your supermarket, you may want to think about buying it for some meatballs. Veal produces super-tender, juicy meatballs, and contains more collagen than other ground meats, meaning you can use fewer breadcrumbs and binders. It's perfect for mixing with other meats, but the Veal Meatballs with Gravy on page 90 give you an opportunity to taste the delicacy of a veal-only meatball if you wish.

Pork. Pork completes the trifecta of meats (beef, veal, and pork) that are commonly found in meatballs—often all together! While many feel the fat and flavor in pork perfectly complements beef, many Asian meatball recipes contain pork only. (Try the Garlic-Ginger Porkball Soup on page 62, which contains meatballs made by simply squeezing bits of ground pork into broth.)

Lamb. Popular in Mediterranean recipes, meatballs made with lamb are a decadent treat. Ground lamb is often sold frozen, though fresh ground lamb can sometimes be found in organic grocery stores and at Middle Eastern (halal)

butcher shops. Because lamb is so flavorful, it can stand up to lots of spices and is often accented with lemon, mint, and other seasonings that can cut through the lamb's heartiness (like in the Lamb Kofta with Tzatziki Sauce on page 37).

Chicken and Turkey. If red meat isn't really your thing, your kids only eat chicken, or you're looking to save a few calories, chicken and turkey meatballs have a lot going for them. They also showcase other flavors well, like in the Buffalo Chicken Meatballs on page 102 and the Turkey Meatballs with Couscous on page 108. When selecting ground chicken or turkey at the market, make sure not to go too lean—select a mix that's not just white meat, and try to use meat that's at least 10 percent fat (90 percent lean or lower).

Sausage. While not an individual meat on its own, of course, sausage is made from one of the above meats, seasoned, and then either sold as "bulk sausage" or put into casings. An easy way to add flavor to your meatballs is to substitute sausage for plain ground meat. Sausage is easy to remove from its casing, especially when it's locally made. Just squeeze out one side into the bowl. And oftentimes, it's easier to find ground pork, turkey, and chicken in sausage form than plain. The Spicy Red Pepper Meatballs on page 86, for instance, use andouille sausage to give them a nice kick.

Fish. When is a meatball not a meatball? When it's a fishball! Balls of fish are a traditional part of Asian cuisine, and

they're easy to make if you use a flaky fish or have a food processor. After trying out the Pan-Fried Salmon Balls on page 136 and the Shrimp Balls with Ginger-Soy Sauce on page 139 you might have a new favorite meatball.

OTHER MEATBALL INGREDIENTS

Meatballs are pretty simple, but if you've ever made them before, you know they're not just meat in ball form. Here are the other ingredients commonly used in a typical meatball, no matter what kind of meat you use.

Breadcrumbs. Most (but not all) meatball recipes contain bread or cracker crumbs. Breadcrumbs not only make the texture of meatballs lighter and fluffier, they also help hold them together. That's because the crumbs soak up any added moisture (see "Binders" below) and become sticky, keeping the ground meat from falling apart while you're cooking it. Breadcrumbs can take a lot of forms, from the traditional variety (plain or Italian-seasoned) to crushed-up crackers to Japanese panko crumbs made from bread with the crusts removed (and used in such recipes as the Pork Meatball Bành Mìs on page 72).

Many cooks swear by making their own breadcrumbs for meatballs—their coarser texture helps the meat stay together better. For even softer meatballs, use the Martha Stewart-approved method: fresh bread torn into pieces and

soaked in milk, like in the Classic Italian Meatballs on page 80. If you want your meatballs to have a crispy crust (like the Sausage-Stuffed Rice Balls on page 46), after forming them dredge them in flour, egg, and breadcrumbs.

Gluten-free meatballs. If you're on a gluten-free diet, meatballs are great option for you! Just substitute any bread or breadcrumbs with gluten-free versions, which are available at most health-food stores. You can also try omitting the breadcrumbs entirely, but you may have to play around with the recipe a bit and reduce some of the liquid to get the right consistency. Make sure to check the rest of the ingredients in the meatball (like soy sauce or ketchup) to make sure they're gluten-free.

Binders. Binders go hand in hand with breadcrumbs to help your tiny culinary creations stay in one piece. A lightly beaten egg and milk are two common ones used throughout this book, but you can also just use water to moisten the bread. Cheese (as long as you don't use too much) can also make a great binder. Meatballs that are formed around skewers (like the Chicken Kebabs on page 140) need fewer binders.

Seasonings. What makes a meatball unique is what kinds of seasonings go inside. Just about every meatball recipe contains salt and black pepper, and many contain garlic

and onions, but they diverge wildly from there. Herbs like oregano, basil, and thyme are a popular choice for seasoning meatballs, especially those with Italian roots. Swedish and Middle Eastern-inspired meatballs use the fragrant flavors of cloves, cinnamon, and nutmeg. Many other meatball recipes in this book contain Mexican spices, Asian condiments like soy sauce, or American touches like salad dressing. You'll find meatballs that contain fruits and vegetables like spinach, red peppers, mushrooms, or raisins; nuts like pine nuts or pecans; even whole olives or entire hard-boiled eggs. What will your house recipe meatballs include?

MEATBALL ACCOMPANIMENTS

When you're done with a batch of meatballs, it's virtually impossible not to pop one or two in your mouth and eat them right away. But for the most part, a meatball needs an accompaniment. This can just be a tasty sauce (like many of the recipes in the Appetizers chapter), a starch like pasta or rice, or both! Since a meatball shouldn't stand alone, this book is full of sauces, starches, and even some soups and sandwiches you can pair with your meatballs. Suggestions for mixing and matching are included throughout!

Meatball-Making Mastery

Now that you know everything that goes into a meatball, what do you do with all these ingredients? Mixing together meatballs is a job best done with your hands—just make sure to wash them thoroughly before and after. Get your hands wet to keep the ground meat from sticking to them, then just dive right in and smush the meat and seasonings between your fingers. If you hate the sensation of mixing meat together and are buying different kinds (for instance, beef, pork, and veal), you can ask the butcher to combine them for you. You can also try wearing disposable latex gloves or using a big wooden spoon.

Whether you mind hand-mixing meat or not, don't spend too long combining everything together: the more loosely packed your meatball is, the lighter it will be. (This is because the meatball will have more tiny air pockets inside.) Thanks to your binder, you'll be sure they stick together!

The size of your meatball will vary based on the recipe, and what kind of dish you'll be using them for. Appetizer and soup meatballs are better bite-sized (about ¾-1 inch in diameter), while main-dish meatballs are usually around 2 inches in diameter. If you're making a bigger meatball than that, it should be one that's braised (simmered in sauce or liquid) to make sure it cooks fully and evenly. No matter how big your meatballs, try to make them all the same size to ensure they all cook in the same amount of time.

To shape the meatballs, you can use your hands, a special meatball scoop (available at kitchen stores), or an ice

cream scoop. If you have time, cover the raw meatballs and stick them in the refrigerator for 15 minutes, which will help them keep their shape better when cooking by stiffening the fats in the meat and giving the binders time to work.

Cooking Your Meatballs

Like mixing and matching meats, spices, and sauces, you can also pick your favorite way to prepare meatballs and make it your dinnertime go-to. Some meals lend themselves to certain ways of making meatballs (if you're making spaghetti sauce, for instance, it's a shame to not throw the meatballs right into the sauce to cook), and the recipes in this book reflect the cooking method best suited to that dish or traditional to that cuisine. Here's an overview of each method with some helpful hints to make them even easier.

BROWNING

Most meatball recipes include a browning step, when you sauté the meatballs in a small amount of oil to get them brown on all sides. This isn't meant to cook the meatball all the way through, but to help it keep its shape, give it some good color, and even make it juicer. Use tongs or a spatula to turn the meatballs every 2-3 minutes as they cook over medium-high heat in a tablespoon of olive or canola oil. Cook them in batches if they don't all fit in the pan; if they're too close together they'll steam instead of sear. If your meatballs tend to look not-so-round by the time you're done with the browning stage, don't worry—no one judges a meatball by shape rather than taste! After you've quickly browned the meatball on as many sides as possible, switch to another (usually slower) cooking method to fully cook their insides.

BAKING

Baking is an easy (and delicious!) way to cook lots of meatballs at once, and is used in many of the recipes in this book. Baking time and temperatures vary based on the meat and size of your meatball, but they all involve placing the meatballs on a baking sheet after browning and baking until cooked through. To make the meatballs heat more evenly and to let all the excess fat drip off of them, elevate them slightly off the baking sheet with a wire rack. If you don't have a suitable baking rack, you can use a metal cookie cooling rack or even the wire rack from your toaster oven (if it's removable). Just thoroughly wash it before returning it to its original purpose.

BRAISING

Braising is slowly cooking a food in a sauce or liquid, and meatballs are one of the most commonly braised dinners! If you've ever had a meatball slow-cooked in marinara (like the ones on page 83), you know what a delicious taste braising liquid can impart to a meatball. Some of the unique versions in this book include Meatballs in Mushroom Sauce on page 116, and the soups on pages 52-67.

FRYING

If you love a super-crispy outer shell on your meatballs, you'll love the taste of a fried meatball. Some meatball recipes (like the Fried Pork Meatballs on page 95) call for deep-frying the meatballs by covering them with oil on the stovetop or in a deep-fryer. But many (like the Swedish Meatballs on page 92) simply prolong the browning step, sautéing the meatballs on the stove until they're completely cooked through. Place them on paper towels afterward to allow excess oil to drain while they cool.

GRILLING

If you live behind your grill in the summertime or have a stovetop grill pan you love to use, there are plenty of meatball recipes for you. Traditional meatball recipes from the Middle East (like the Chicken Kebabs on page 140) are shaped around skewers, forming a log-like shape. Then there are the American-style meatballs speared with veggies, like in the Meatball Shish Kebabs on page 105. There's also a handy device called a meatball basket that you can buy especially for your barbecue—just spray it with some cooking spray and put the meatballs inside before putting on the grill.

Meatball Leftovers

Saving meatballs for later is easy, so make sure to make twice as many as you need and you'll have an easy meal later! After forming the raw meatballs, place them in a resealable plastic bag and lay it flat in the freezer. Once frozen, you can stash the bag standing up in the freezer for up to a month or more. Then simply thaw in the fridge or microwave and pick up right where you left off in the recipe. If you're frying them, you don't even have to wait for them to thaw! Just add a few extra minutes to the frying time.

    If the meatballs are already cooked, the best method for reheating them is in the oven (bake uncovered at 375°F for 15-20 minutes). Or better yet, reheat them in their braising sauce. Meatballs in marinara (like one of the recipes on pages 80-83) and meatball soup also freeze well—once you've reheated them you'll never be able to tell they weren't freshly made.

Meatballs Are for Lovers

They're easy to make, completely customizable, and encompass cuisines from across the globe. But one of the best things about meatballs is how easy they are to share. Whether you're making hors d'oeuvres for a party, meatballs in sauce for a family dinner, or an exotic meatball dish for a potluck, you'll find people always gravitate toward a plate of meatballs. Enjoy!

APPETIZERS

MEATBALLS with SPICY DIPPING SAUCE

●●●

These delectable appetizers take the meatballs off the pasta and put them onto your party spread. If you don't prefer your sauce spicy, just omit the sriracha chili sauce and cayenne pepper.

SPICY DIPPING SAUCE

1 tablespoon olive oil
½ of 1 medium onion, finely chopped
2 garlic cloves, minced
1 (14.5 ounce) can crushed tomatoes
2-3 teaspoons (to taste) sriracha chili sauce
½ teaspoon cayenne pepper
1 tablespoon fresh parsley, chopped
½ teaspoon salt
¼ teaspoon black pepper

MEATBALLS

1 pound ground beef
½ pound ground pork
1 large onion, finely chopped
½ cup breadcrumbs
1 large egg, lightly beaten
½ cup milk
1 tablespoon fresh parsley, chopped
1 teaspoon ground cumin
2 teaspoons salt
1 teaspoon black pepper

1. In large saucepan, heat oil over medium-high heat. Add onions and cook, stirring, for 2 minutes; add garlic and continue to cook until onions are translucent and garlic is tender, about 2-3 minutes more.

2. Add tomatoes, sriracha sauce, cayenne pepper, parsley, salt, and pepper. Bring to a boil, then reduce heat to medium low and cook for at least 15 minutes.

3. Meanwhile, loosely mix together beef, pork, onion, breadcrumbs, egg, milk, parsley, cumin, salt, and pepper, and form into balls about 1 inch in diameter.

4. Heat oil over medium-high heat, then add meatballs (in batches if necessary), turning two or three times during cooking time, until browned, about 6-8 minutes.

5. Turn heat down to medium and continue to turn while cooking until cooked through, about 10 minutes. Drain on paper towels. Serve with sauce.

BARBECUE MEATBALLS

●●●

Make these mini masterpieces and you'll quickly discover that very few people turn down barbecue meatballs at a party. These lovely little treats are small and smothered in sauce, so they don't even need to be pan-fried, making this recipe super easy, too.

BARBECUE SAUCE

2 cups ketchup
¾ cup chicken stock or water
½ cup apple cider vinegar
¼ cup dark brown sugar
¼ cup sugar
1 tablespoon honey mustard
1 tablespoon Worcestershire sauce
2 teaspoons garlic powder
1 teaspoon onion powder
1 teaspoon salt
1 teaspoon black pepper

MEATBALLS

1 pound ground beef
½ pound ground pork
1 large onion, finely chopped
1 cup quick-cooking oats
1 large egg, lightly beaten
½ cup milk
1 teaspoon cayenne pepper
1½ teaspoons salt
½ teaspoon black pepper

1. In a large saucepan, combine ketchup, chicken stock or water, apple cider vinegar, brown sugar, sugar, honey mustard, Worcestershire sauce, garlic powder, onion powder, salt, and pepper, and bring to a boil over medium-high heat.

2. Reduce heat to low and simmer, uncovered, stirring occasionally until thickened and reduced to approximately 2 cups of sauce, about 1 hour.

3. Preheat oven to 350°F.

4. Loosely mix together beef, pork, onion, oats, egg, milk, cayenne pepper, salt, and pepper. Shape mixture into balls approximately ¾ inch to 1 inch in diameter and place in a single layer in a 13 x 9-inch pan.

5. Pour 1½ cups barbecue sauce over meatballs and bake for 20 minutes. Top with remaining sauce and bake until cooked through, approximately 10-15 minutes more.

CHEDDAR CHEESE MEATBALLS

● ● ●

These all-beef appetizer meatballs have a surprise hidden inside: a hunk of Cheddar cheese. What could be better? Use an oven-safe skillet on the stove so you can just pop it in the oven to finish cooking the meatballs.

2 pounds ground beef
1 medium onion, finely chopped
3 garlic cloves, minced
¼ cup breadcrumbs
1 large egg, lightly beaten
1 teaspoon chili powder
2 teaspoons salt
1 teaspoon black pepper
½ pound Cheddar cheese, cut into ½-inch cubes
1 tablespoon vegetable or olive oil

1. Preheat oven to 450°F.

2. Loosely mix together beef, onion, garlic, breadcrumbs, onion, egg, chili powder, salt, and pepper.

3. Wrap each cheese cube with meat mixture, forming meatballs about 1½ inch in diameter.

4. Heat oil in an oven-safe skillet over medium-high heat, then add meatballs (in batches if necessary), turning two or three times during cooking time, until browned but not cooked through, about 6-8 minutes.

5. Place the skillet in the oven and bake until meatballs are cooked through, about 10-15 minutes. Drain on paper towels. Serve with ketchup or another dipping sauce.

MIX 'N' MATCH

These Southwestern-inspired meatballs taste great with the Salsa Verde on page 98.

MEATBALLS with SWEET and SOUR SAUCE

●●●

These lip-smacking hors d'oeuvres are so tasty, it's impossible to eat just one. The spices in both the meatballs and the sauce balance acidity with sweetness, and are reminiscent of a tangy, Carolina-style barbecue sauce.

SWEET AND SOUR SAUCE

⅓ cup water
1 cup pineapple juice
3 tablespoons apple cider vinegar
1 tablespoon soy sauce
½ cup packed brown sugar
3 tablespoons cornstarch

MEATBALLS

½ pound ground beef
½ pound ground pork
1½ teaspoons Worcestershire sauce
½ teaspoon mustard
1 garlic clove, minced
¼ cup breadcrumbs
1 large egg, lightly beaten
1 teaspoon salt
½ teaspoon black pepper
1 tablespoon vegetable or olive oil

1. In medium saucepan, combine water, pineapple juice, apple cider vinegar, soy sauce, brown sugar, and cornstarch. Heat over medium heat, stirring frequently, until bubbly, thickened, and heated through, about 10 minutes.

2. Loosely mix together beef, pork, Worcestershire sauce, mustard, garlic, breadcrumbs, egg, salt, and pepper. Shape into balls about 1 inch in diameter.

3. Heat oil in skillet over medium-high heat, then add meatballs, turning two or three times during cooking time, until browned, about 6-8 minutes.

4. Turn heat down to medium and continue to turn while cooking until cooked through, about 10 minutes.

5. Remove from heat and drain on paper towels. Serve with sweet and sour sauce.

TERIYAKI MEATBALLS

● ● ●

Inside these zesty, Asian-inspired meatballs is an ingredient you may not be familiar with: panko breadcrumbs. From Japan, panko breadcrumbs are just like traditional breadcrumbs made from white bread, but without the crusts. This makes them lighter and fluffier—and perfect for meatballs. If you don't see them in your grocery store's ethnic food aisle or breadcrumb section, you can always substitute traditional breadcrumbs.

1 pound ground beef
1 pound ground turkey
4 scallions, diced
3 garlic cloves, minced
½ teaspoon fresh ginger, minced
½ cup panko breadcrumbs
1 large egg, lightly beaten
1 tablespoon soy sauce
1 teaspoon sesame oil
½ teaspoon black pepper
1 tablespoon olive oil
1 cup teriyaki marinade

1. Loosely mix together beef, turkey, scallions, garlic, ginger, panko breadcrumbs, egg, soy sauce, sesame oil, and pepper. Shape into balls about 1 inch in diameter.

2. Heat oil in saucepan over medium-high heat, then add meatballs (in batches if necessary), turning two or three times during cooking time, until browned, about 6-8 minutes.

3. If you cooked in batches, return all meatballs to saucepan with teriyaki marinade and simmer, covered, over medium heat until meatballs are cooked through, about 10 minutes.

MIX 'N' MATCH

These meatballs also taste great with the Ginger-Soy dipping sauce on page 139! Just skip step 3 and continue to sauté in the pan until cooked though, about 10 additional minutes.

BEEF FALAFEL

●●●

This twist on falafel is made with bulgur, super-healthy wheat kernels packed with nutrients and found in traditional Middle Eastern tabbouleh salads. For a vegetarian version of this recipe, check out the Falafel Sandwiches on page 77.

1½ cups bulgur wheat
3 cups water
1 pound ground beef
3 garlic cloves, minced
2 teaspoons ground cumin
1½ teaspoons ground coriander
1 tablespoon fresh mint leaves, chopped
1 teaspoon salt
¼ teaspoon pepper
2 tablespoons olive oil

1. In medium saucepan, combine bulgur and water and bring to a boil. Cover, reduce heat to low, and simmer until bulgur is tender, about 10-12 minutes. Drain.

2. Preheat oven to 425°F.

3. Mix together bulgur, beef, garlic, cumin, coriander, mint, salt, and pepper. Shape into balls about 1 inch in diameter. Brush on all sides with oil.

4. Place on baking sheets and bake until cooked through, about 10-15 minutes.

MIX 'N' MATCH!

These beef falafel are perfect with hummus, but they also go great with the Tzatziki Sauce on page 37!

LAMB KOFTA with TZATZIKI SAUCE

●●●

Cooked with skewers on the grill, these log-shaped meatballs (called "kofta") are perfect for summer—especially if you have fresh herbs in your garden. Mint gives them a nice zing that's perfectly paired with a refreshing Greek tzatziki sauce. Serve them on toothpicks as an appetizer, then eat the leftovers in a pita with some tomato and lettuce!

MEATBALLS

1 pound ground lamb
1 small onion, finely chopped
1 garlic clove, minced
1 large egg, lightly beaten
2 tablespoons breadcrumbs
1 tablespoon mayonnaise

½ cup fresh mint, chopped
3 tablespoons fresh parsley, chopped
½ teaspoon cinnamon
1 teaspoon salt
½ teaspoon black pepper

TZATZIKI SAUCE

1 medium cucumber
2 teaspoons salt
1 cup plain Greek yogurt
1 garlic clove, minced
2 teaspoons lemon juice
¼ teaspoon black pepper
1 teaspoon fresh mint, chopped (optional)

1. Loosely mix together all meatball ingredients and shape into 2-inch ovals around the pointy end of each skewer, so that it forms a log shape that just covers the skewer's point.

2. Heat a grill pan or barbecue grill over medium heat, then grill the meatballs (working in batches if necessary), turning two or three times until brown all over and cooked through, about 6 minutes.

3. To make the tzatziki sauce, peel cucumber and scoop out seeds with a spoon. Grate it with a box grater, then add to a sieve. Sprinkle with salt and let liquid drain from the cucumbers for 20 minutes. Squeeze to get out any remaining liquid.

4. Add cucumber to yogurt along with garlic, lemon juice, black pepper, and mint (optional). Cover and refrigerate for at least 30 minutes.

FRIED THANKSGIVING STUFFING BALLS

●●●

If stuffing is your favorite food at Thanksgiving time, you'll absolutely love these fried balls of joy. These are perfect to make with leftover stuffing, but they're a big hit year-round. Substitute some cooked, bulk sausage for the dried cranberries or pecans if you'd like a meatier bite!

> ¼ cup (½ stick) butter or margarine
> 1 large onion, finely chopped
> 2 stalks celery, diced
> 2½ cups chicken broth
> 1 (14 ounce) package seasoned stuffing mix
> 1 large egg, lightly beaten
> 1 cup dried, sweetened cranberries
> 1 cup chopped pecans
> Oil for frying

1. Preheat oven to 350°F.

2. In a medium saucepan, melt butter over medium-high heat. Add onion and celery and cook, stirring, until translucent, about 6-8 minutes. Remove from heat.

3. Add chicken broth, then stuffing mix, egg, cranberries, and pecans. Shape into balls about 1 inch in diameter. If mixture is too dry, add water or more broth.

4. Heat oil in deep-fryer or in a large pot (about 2½ inches deep) on the stovetop to 350°F. Fry stuffing balls in batches until golden brown, about 3 minutes. Let drain on paper towels.

MIX 'N' MATCH

Fried Thanksgiving Stuffing Balls are perfect alone, but for a treat, you can serve them with the Traditional Gravy on page 90.

HAM and CHEESE CROQUETTES

● ● ●

These balls have meat in them, but they're far from your traditional meatball. A major player at sophisticated parties, ham and cheese croquettes are made by cooling béchamel sauce, also known as white sauce—so make sure to give yourself enough time (and space) to refrigerate the sauce until it's the proper consistency. If you can't find fontina cheese to complement the ham, you can substitute Gouda or Gruyere.

¼ cup (½ stick) butter or margarine
1 medium onion, finely chopped
1 garlic clove, minced
½ cup all-purpose flour
½ teaspoon salt
½ teaspoon pepper
¾ cup milk (preferably whole)
6 tablespoons finely chopped ham
¾ cup shredded fontina cheese
½ cup Parmesan cheese
1½ cups breadcrumbs
3 large eggs, beaten
Oil, for frying

1. Heat butter in saucepan over medium heat until melted. Add onion and garlic and cook, stirring occasionally, until onion is translucent, about 3 minutes.

2. Add flour, salt, and pepper and cook, stirring constantly, until mixture is dry and stiff, about 1-2 minutes.

3. Continuing to heat over medium heat, gradually mix in milk with a whisk until smooth, about 3 minutes. Stir in ham and fontina cheese.

4. Spread mixture onto a baking sheet and cool. Then cover with plastic wrap or waxed paper and refrigerate until firm, at least 45 minutes but up to a day.

5. In dish or bowl suitable for dipping, mix together Parmesan cheese and breadcrumbs. In separate dish, whisk together eggs.

6. With floured hands, shape ham-fontina mixture into ovals about 2 inches long.

7. Dip each oval into eggs, then breadcrumb mixture.

8. Heat oil in deep-fryer or in a large pot (about 2½ inches deep) on the stovetop to 375°F. Fry croquettes in batches until golden brown, about 1-2 minutes. Let drain on paper towels.

MASHED POTATO CROQUETTES with BACON

● ● ●

These country cousins of the Ham and Cheese Croquettes on page 40 are simple to make and couldn't be more delicious. Perfect to make with leftover mashed potatoes, they taste like a bite-sized loaded baked potato! Serve them with sour cream to complete the dish.

> 2 cups mashed potatoes, cooled
> 2 egg yolks from large eggs
> 3 strips bacon, cooked and crumbled
> 1 scallion, chopped
> 1 teaspoon black pepper
> ½ cup all-purpose flour
> 1 large egg, beaten
> 1 cup breadcrumbs
> Oil for frying

1. Mix together mashed potatoes, egg yolks, bacon, scallions, and pepper.

2. Shape into balls about 1 inch in diameter, then dip each ball into flour, then beaten egg, then breadcrumbs.

3. Heat oil in deep-fryer or in a large pot (about 2½ inches deep) on the stovetop to 350°F. Fry mashed potato croquettes in batches until golden brown, about 2 minutes. Let drain on paper towels.

MIX 'N' MATCH

Inside of serving with sour cream, try these Mashed Potato Croquettes with the Cheese Sauce on page 115!

VEGETARIAN RICE BALLS

●●●

Rice balls are even more Italian than meatballs, and worth mastering for the happiness they bring when someone takes their first warm-and-delicious bite. Rice balls are made from risotto, which can seem intimidating to make, but is easier than you think. Just make sure to use Arborio rice and warmed broth, and commit to standing at your stove for a little while to continuously stir the rice while it's cooking.

RISOTTO

2 tablespoons butter
1 medium onion, finely chopped
3 garlic cloves, minced
1½ cups Arborio rice
1 cup white wine

4 cups warm vegetable broth
2 cups fresh spinach, chopped
1 cup grated Romano cheese
½ teaspoon salt
¼ teaspoon black pepper

RICE BALLS

½ cup grated Parmesan cheese
1½ cups Italian breadcrumbs
1 cup all-purpose flour

2 large eggs, beaten
Oil for frying

1. In large saucepan, melt butter over medium-high heat. Add onion and cook, stirring, for 2 minutes; add garlic and continue to cook until onions are translucent and garlic is tender, about 2-3 minutes more.

2. Add rice. Cook, stirring occasionally, until rice starts to become fragrant, about 5 minutes. Add wine and continue to cook and stir for 5 minutes.

3. Add half of broth. Cook, stirring, until rice mixture is thick and broth is absorbed, about 10 minutes. Add remaining broth and continue to stir until thickened and absorbed, about 10 more minutes.

4. Add spinach, Romano cheese, salt, and pepper. Mix to combine.

5. Spread risotto onto a baking sheet and cool. Then cover with plastic wrap or waxed paper and refrigerate overnight or until firm.

6. Shape risotto into balls about 1½ inches in diameter.

7. In dish or bowl suitable for dipping, mix together Parmesan cheese and breadcrumbs.

8. Dip each ball into flour, then eggs, then breadcrumb mixture.

9. Heat oil in deep-fryer or in a large pot (about 2½ inches deep) on the stovetop to 350°F. Fry rice balls in batches until golden brown, about 1-2 minutes. Let drain on paper towels.

SAUSAGE-STUFFED RICE BALLS

● ● ●

Meatball/rice ball hybrids, these mouthwatering Italian appetizers are also perfect for reheating in the oven as afterschool snacks for the kids. Use the Risotto recipe from the Vegetarian Rice Balls on page 44 if you don't have your own.

3 cups cooked risotto
½ pound bulk pork sausage
1 small onion, finely chopped
2 garlic cloves, minced
1 (8 ounce) can tomato sauce
1 teaspoon tomato paste
1 teaspoon dried oregano
½ teaspoon salt
¼ teaspoon black pepper
1 cup all-purpose flour
1 large egg, beaten
1 cup Italian breadcrumbs
Oil for frying

1. Spread risotto onto a baking sheet and cool. Then cover with plastic wrap or waxed paper and refrigerate overnight or until firm.

2. Cook sausage in skillet over medium-high heat, stirring and breaking up, until cooked through but not browned, about 6 minutes. Add onion and garlic and cook until onion is translucent and sausage is browned, about 3 minutes more. Drain off fat.

3. Add tomato sauce, tomato paste, oregano, salt, and pepper. Continue to cook over medium-high heat, stirring occasionally, until sauce thickens slightly, about 8-10 minutes. Remove from heat.

4. Shape risotto into balls about 1½ inches in diameter. Make a well in the center of each ball and drop approximately 1 tablespoon of sausage mixture inside. Then work the rice over the well so that it completely encloses the sausage, smoothing back into a ball shape if necessary.

5. Dip each ball into flour, then eggs, then breadcrumbs.

6. Heat oil in deep-fryer or in a large pot (about 2½ inches deep) on the stovetop to about 350°F. Fry rice balls in batches until golden brown, about 1-2 minutes. Let drain on paper towels.

MEATBALL PIZZA

●●●

Meatballs are perfect for pizza, and pizza is perfect for a family dinner that the kids can help you make. Buy pre-made pizza dough at the supermarket, or ask to buy dough at your favorite pizza parlor—they're usually willing to oblige!

MEATBALLS

½ pound ground beef
1 garlic clove, minced
2 tablespoons breadcrumbs
2 tablespoons grated
  Parmesan cheese
1 tablespoon fresh basil, chopped
½ teaspoon salt
¼ teaspoon black pepper
1 tablespoon water
1 tablespoon olive oil

PIZZA

1 small onion, chopped
½ bell pepper, chopped
20 cherry or grape tomatoes
1 tablespoon olive oil
1 round of pizza dough
1 tablespoon olive oil
1 cup pizza sauce
1 (8 ounce) package mozzarella
  cheese, shredded
½ of 1 (4.5 ounce) jar mushrooms,
  drained

1. Preheat oven to 450°F.

2. Loosely mix together beef, garlic, breadcrumbs, Parmesan cheese, basil, salt, pepper, and water. Shape mixture into balls about ¾ inch in diameter.

3. Heat oil in skillet over medium-high heat, then add meatballs (in batches if necessary), turning during cooking time, until browned but not cooked through, about 3-5 minutes. Remove meatballs to baking sheet.

4. Add onion and bell pepper to hot oil and cook until soft, about 6 minutes. Cover and set aside.

5. Meanwhile, add tomatoes to baking sheet with meatballs and place in the oven. Bake until tomatoes are blistered and meatballs are cooked through, about 10 minutes. When slightly cooled, slice meatballs in half.

6. Stretch pizza dough into pan and brush olive oil on top. Add pizza sauce and mozzarella cheese, then top with mushrooms, bell pepper, onions, and meatballs.

7. Cook until crust is golden brown and cheese is bubbling, about 10 minutes.

SOUPS *and* SANDWICHES

ITALIAN WEDDING SOUP

● ● ●

This chicken broth-based soup is perfect for the still-chilly early days of spring, because it's both hearty and light at the same time. The meatballs take center stage, backed up by carrots and potatoes. Top off each bowl with an extra grating of Parmesan cheese.

MEATBALLS

½ pound ground beef
½ pound ground pork
1 small onion, finely chopped
1 garlic clove, minced
1 slice white bread, crust trimmed, torn into small pieces

¼ cup milk
1 large egg, lightly beaten
½ cup grated Parmesan cheese
½ teaspoon salt
½ teaspoon black pepper
1 tablespoon olive oil

SOUP

6 cups chicken broth
1 Yukon Gold potato, peeled and chopped into bite-sized pieces
2 medium carrots, peeled and chopped into bite-sized pieces
1 dried bay leaf
1½ teaspoons dried thyme
1 teaspoon dried basil
1 teaspoon black pepper

1. Loosely mix together beef, pork, onion, garlic, bread, milk, egg, Parmesan cheese, salt, and pepper. Shape into balls about 1 inch in diameter. Cover and set aside.

2. In a large pot, bring broth to boil over medium-high heat. Reduce heat to medium-low and add potatoes, carrots, and bay leaf. Let simmer until potatoes and carrots are almost tender, about 10-15 minutes.

3. Meanwhile, heat oil in skillet over medium-high heat, then add meatballs (in batches if necessary), turning during cooking time, until browned but not cooked through, about 3-5 minutes.

4. When potatoes and carrots are almost cooked through, add meatballs, thyme, basil, and pepper. Simmer until meatballs are cooked through and vegetables are tender, about 10 minutes. Remove bay leaf before serving.

BEEFY MEATBALL STEW

●●●

Save bones from spare ribs, roasts, or other beef dishes to make this robust stew even better. Simply omit the flour and add the bones (with any meat attached) instead. They will thicken the soup stew and add to its rich flavor.

MEATBALLS

½ pound ground beef
½ pound ground veal
1 garlic clove, minced
2 tablespoons breadcrumbs
1 tablespoon ketchup

1 large egg, lightly beaten
1 teaspoon salt
½ teaspoon black pepper
1 tablespoon olive oil

SOUP

1 large onion, diced
2 medium carrots, peeled and chopped into bite-sized pieces
3 garlic cloves, minced
2 tablespoons all-purpose flour
1 tablespoon tomato paste
5 cups beef broth
1 (14.5 ounce) can fire-roasted diced tomatoes

1 dried bay leaf
2 tablespoons Worcestershire sauce
1 teaspoon dried rosemary
½ teaspoon salt
1 teaspoon black pepper
½ of 1 (16 ounce) package conchiglie (small shell) pasta, cooked

1. Loosely mix together beef, veal, garlic, breadcrumbs, ketchup, egg, salt, and pepper. Shape into balls about 1 inch in diameter.

2. Heat oil in large saucepan over medium-high heat, then add meatballs (in batches if necessary), turning during cooking time, until browned but not cooked through, about 6-8 minutes. Remove meatballs with slotted spoon and set aside, covered.

3. Add onions and carrots to hot oil. Cook until they start to soften, about 5-7 minutes. Add garlic and cook until onion is translucent, about 2 minutes more.

4. Add flour and stir until vegetable mixture is coated. Add tomato paste and stir until incorporated.

5. Add broth, tomatoes, bay leaf, Worcestershire sauce, rosemary, salt, pepper, and meatballs. Bring to a boil, then reduce heat to medium-low and simmer until meatballs and carrots are cooked through, about 10-15 minutes. Remove bay leaf and stir in cooked pasta before serving.

CHICKEN MEATBALL SOUP

●●●

Dress up ramen noodles in this ingenious dish made with chicken meatballs. It's so quick and tasty that it might surpass traditional chicken soup as your sick-day go-to.

MEATBALLS

1 pound ground chicken (light and dark mix)
2 garlic cloves, minced
2 tablespoons panko breadcrumbs
2 teaspoons poultry seasoning
1 large egg, lightly beaten
1 teaspoon salt
½ teaspoon black pepper
1 tablespoon olive oil

SOUP

1 medium onion, diced
2 medium carrots, grated
3 garlic cloves, diced
4 cups reduced-sodium chicken stock
2 cups water
1 bay leaf
3 (3-ounce) packages chicken-flavored
   ramen noodles with seasoning packet
3 scallions, chopped, for garnish

1. Loosely mix together chicken, garlic, panko breadcrumbs, poultry seasoning, egg, salt, and pepper. Shape into balls about 1 inch in diameter.

2. Heat oil in large saucepan over medium-high heat, then add meatballs (in batches if necessary), turning during cooking time, until browned but not cooked through, about 3 minutes. Remove meatballs with slotted spoon and set aside, covered.

3. Add onion and carrots to hot oil. Cook until onion starts to soften, about 3-5 minutes. Add garlic and cook until onion is translucent and carrot is soft, about 2 minutes more.

4. Add chicken stock, water, bay leaf, ramen noodle seasoning packets, and meatballs and bring to a boil. Reduce heat to medium-low and simmer until meatballs are cooked through, about 8-10 minutes.

5. Add ramen noodles and simmer until tender, about 3 minutes. Remove bay leaf before serving and garnish with chopped scallions.

ALBÓNDIGAS SOUP

●●●

This traditional Mexican soup gets its deep smoky flavor from chipotle chilies, which you've probably heard of (thanks to the popular restaurant chain), but might not have ever cooked with. You can find chipotles at Mexican grocery stores or in the ethnic aisle of your grocery store. They come in small cans packed in a delicious sauce that's also used in this recipe.

MEATBALLS

⅔ pound ground beef

⅓ pound bulk chorizo or link chorizo with its casings removed

1 clove garlic, minced

¼ cup crushed corn tortilla chips

¼ cup grated zucchini

1 large egg, lightly beaten

1 tablespoon fresh cilantro, chopped

1 teaspoon ground cumin

½ teaspoon dried oregano

1 teaspoon salt

½ teaspoon black pepper

1 tablespoon olive oil

SOUP

1 medium onion, diced

1 large carrot, grated

3 garlic cloves, diced

5 cups chicken or beef stock

1 chipotle chili, chopped, plus 1 teaspoon sauce from 1 can of chipotle chilies in adobo sauce

1 (28 ounce) can crushed tomatoes

½ teaspoon dried oregano

½ teaspoon ground cumin

1 teaspoon salt

½ teaspoon black pepper

¼ cup uncooked rice

3 scallions, chopped, for garnish

1. Loosely mix together beef, chorizo, garlic, tortilla chips, zucchini, egg, cilantro, cumin, oregano, salt, and pepper. Shape into balls about 1 inch in diameter.

2. Heat oil in large pot over medium-high heat, then add meatballs (in batches if necessary), turning during cooking time, until browned but not cooked through, about 3 minutes. Remove meatballs with slotted spoon and set aside, covered.

3. Add onion and carrot to hot oil. Cook until they start to soften, about 5-7 minutes. Add garlic and cook until onion is translucent and carrot is soft, about 2 minutes more.

4. Add chicken or beef stock, chipotle chili and sauce, tomatoes, oregano, cumin, salt, pepper, and rice. Cook until rice is tender, about 20-30 minutes. Add meatballs back in 10 minutes before end of cooking time. Garnish with chopped scallions before serving.

LENTIL SOUP
with LAMB BALLS

● ● ●

Lentil soup is so old that it was eaten by the ancient Greeks and was even mentioned in the Bible (though some translations simply call it "a mess of pottage"). Though their versions assuredly didn't contain meatballs, lamb is a natural (and scrumptious!) addition to this classic dish. Add a dollop of Greek yogurt on top for the perfect garnish.

MEATBALLS

1 pound ground lamb
1 medium onion, diced
3 garlic cloves, minced
¼ cup breadcrumbs
1 large egg, lightly beaten
2 teaspoons lemon juice

1 cup almonds, toasted and finely chopped
1 medium carrot, grated
2 tablespoons fresh cilantro, chopped
1 teaspoon salt
½ teaspoon black pepper
1 tablespoon olive oil

SOUP

2 tablespoons olive oil
1 large onion, chopped
1 carrot, chopped into bite-sized pieces
4 garlic cloves, diced
6 cups chicken or beef broth

½ cup golden or other dried lentils
2 teaspoons ground cumin
1 teaspoon ground coriander
¼ cup uncooked rice
½ teaspoon salt
¼ teaspoon black pepper

1. In large pot, heat olive oil over medium-high heat. Add onion and carrot to hot oil. Cook until they start to soften, about 5-7 minutes. Add garlic and cook until onion is translucent, about 2 minutes more.

2. Add broth, lentils, cumin, coriander, rice, salt, and pepper. Bring to a boil, then reduce heat to medium-low and simmer until lentils and rice are tender, about 25 minutes.

3. Meanwhile, loosely mix together lamb, onion, garlic, breadcrumbs, egg, lemon juice, almonds, carrot, cilantro, salt, and pepper. Shape into balls about 1 inch in diameter.

4. Heat oil over medium-high heat, then add meatballs, turning two or three times during cooking time, until browned, about 6-8 minutes.

5. Turn heat down to medium and continue to turn while cooking until cooked through, about 10 minutes.

6. Remove from heat and drain on paper towels, then add to individual soup bowls after ladling in soup.

GARLIC-GINGER PORKBALL SOUP

●●●

If you love pork dumplings, you'll love this fresh Asian soup featuring meatballs made of pure pork. Its unconventional (but super-easy) method for adding the meatballs to the soup—pinching them off of a larger log—requires that you refrigerate the mixture to firm it up a bit.

MEATBALLS

1 pound ground pork
3 garlic gloves, minced
1 tablespoon oyster sauce (optional)
1 teaspoon soy sauce
½ teaspoon salt

SOUP

4 cups chicken broth
2 (16 ounce) packages frozen corn
2 garlic cloves, minced
1 tablespoon fresh ginger, minced
½ teaspoon red pepper flakes
2 (14 ounce) cans unsweetened coconut milk
⅓ cup cilantro, chopped, plus more for garnish
2 tablespoons lime juice

1. Mix together the pork, garlic, oyster sauce (optional), soy sauce, and salt. Cover and refrigerate at least 1 hour or overnight.

2. In large pot, heat chicken broth, corn, garlic, ginger, and red pepper flakes over medium-high heat until boiling. Reduce heat to low or medium-low so that soup simmers.

3. Pinch off pieces of the meat mixture one by one and drop into the soup, making bite-sized meatballs about ½ inch in diameter. Cook until meatballs are cooked through, about 2 minutes after dropping the last meatball into the soup.

4. Add coconut milk and cilantro and heat through, about 5 minutes. Stir in lime juice and garnish with cilantro.

PUMPKIN SOUP with TURKEY MEATBALLS

● ● ●

This unique soup uses turkey meatballs to give a pumpkin soup some meaty oomph and flavor. Toasted pumpkin seeds, used for garnish, often go by their Spanish name, *pepitas*, and can be found in Mexican grocery stores or in the bulk section of health-food stores.

MEATBALLS

1 pound ground turkey (light and dark mix)
1 garlic clove, minced
2 tablespoons breadcrumbs
Zest of 1 orange
1 large egg, lightly beaten
1 teaspoon salt
½ teaspoon black pepper
1 tablespoon olive oil

SOUP

2 tablespoons butter
1 small onion, diced
1 garlic clove, minced
2 tablespoons all-purpose flour
6 cups chicken broth
1 (15 ounce) can pumpkin
1 cup sweetened applesauce
½ tablespoon fresh ginger, minced
¼ teaspoon ground nutmeg
1 cup heavy cream
½ cup toasted pumpkin seeds (*pepitas*), for garnish

1. Loosely mix together chicken, garlic, breadcrumbs, orange zest, egg, salt, and pepper. Shape into balls about 1 inch in diameter.

2. Heat oil over medium-high heat, then add meatballs (in batches if necessary), turning two or three times during cooking time, until browned, about 4-6 minutes.

3. Turn heat down to medium and continue to turn while cooking until cooked through, about 10 minutes. Drain on a paper towel and set aside, covered.

4. In a large saucepan, melt butter over medium heat. Add onion and cook until it starts to soften, about 3 minutes. Add garlic and cook until onion is translucent, about 2 minutes more.

5. Add flour and stir until it coats the onion and garlic, about 1 minute. Add broth, pumpkin, applesauce, ginger, and nutmeg and bring to a boil.

6. Reduce heat to low and simmer, covered, for 20 minutes.

7. Add meatballs and heavy cream and cook until the mixture is heated through, about 5 minutes. Garnish with toasted pumpkin seeds.

FISHBALL SOUP

● ● ●

Fishballs are not only a low-fat alternative to meatballs, they're also delicately delicious and perfectly showcased in this Asian soup. They also couldn't be easier to make, as long as you have a food processor. This recipe calls for puréeing white fish—haddock and cod work best.

FISHBALLS

1 pound white fish
¼ cup cold water
2 teaspoons flour
½ teaspoon salt
⅛ teaspoon black pepper

SOUP

4 cups water
2 cups chicken broth
2 medium carrots, peeled and chopped
  into bite-sized pieces
2 tablespoons soy sauce
1 tablespoon sesame oil
1 jalapeño pepper, deseeded and finely chopped
1 tablespoon fresh ginger, minced
3 scallions, roughly chopped

1. Place white fish, water, flour, salt, and pepper in food processor. Blend well. Cover and place in fridge for at least 1 hour and up to 8 hours.

2. In large saucepan, boil water, chicken broth, and carrots over high heat until carrots are tender, about 5 minutes. Reduce heat to medium and add soy sauce, sesame oil, jalapeño, ginger, and scallions. Let simmer for 2 minutes.

3. Shape mixture into balls about 1 inch in diameter and carefully drop into soup. Simmer until cooked through, about 5 minutes.

ITALIAN MEATBALL SUBS

●●●

As quintessential as spaghetti with meatballs is, meatball subs still top many people's lists as the best way to eat meatballs.

MEATBALLS

1 pound ground beef
½ pound ground veal
½ pound bulk sweet Italian sausage, or link sausage with casings removed
1 medium onion, finely chopped
2 garlic cloves, minced

¾ cup Italian breadcrumbs
¼ cup milk
1 large egg, lightly beaten
2 teaspoons salt
1 teaspoon black pepper
1 tablespoon vegetable or olive oil

SAUCE

1 small onion, finely chopped
2 garlic cloves, minced
1 (28 ounce) can crushed tomatoes
1 teaspoon dried thyme
1 teaspoon dried basil or oregano
1 teaspoon salt
1 teaspoon black pepper

SUBS

3-4 French baguettes, halved and ends cut off
1 pound mozzarella cheese, sliced

1. Loosely mix together beef, veal, Italian sausage, onion, garlic, breadcrumbs, milk, egg, salt, and pepper. Shape into balls about 1½ inches in diameter.

2. In large saucepan, heat oil over medium-high heat. Add meatballs (in batches if necessary), turning two or three times during cooking time, until browned, but not cooked through, about 6-8 minutes.

3. Add onion and garlic and cook, stirring occasionally, until onion is translucent, about 3 minutes.

4. Add tomatoes, thyme, basil or oregano, salt, and pepper. If meatballs were cooked in batches, add back in all meatballs.

5. Reduce heat to medium and simmer, covered, until meatballs are cooked through, about 15 minutes.

6. Slice open French bread and lay 2-3 slices of cheese on top. Top with meatballs, sauce, and more cheese. If desired, heat under broiler until cheese melts.

SOUTHWESTERN MEATBALL SLIDERS

●●●

What's better than a burger? A burger you can eat in a few bites! These tasty sliders bring the fun of meatballs to a burger, and have a spicy Southwestern flair.

MEATBALLS

1 pound ground beef
½ pound ground pork
2 garlic cloves, minced
¼ cup breadcrumbs
2 tablespoons milk
1 large egg, lightly beaten
1½ teaspoons ground cumin
1 teaspoon chili powder
1 teaspoon dried oregano
2 teaspoons salt
1 teaspoon black pepper
1 tablespoon vegetable or olive oil

SLIDERS

Approximately 12 dinner rolls
½ pound Cheddar or pepper-jack cheese, sliced
1 medium red onion, sliced
1 tomato, sliced
¼ pound lettuce
1 avocado, peeled and sliced
1 cup salsa

1. Preheat oven to 450°F.

2. Loosely mix together beef, pork, garlic, breadcrumbs, milk, egg, cumin, chili powder, oregano, salt, and pepper. Shape into balls about 2 inches in diameter and flatten slightly.

3. Heat oil in skillet over medium-high heat, then add meatballs (in batches if necessary), turning during cooking time, until browned but not cooked through, about 6-8 minutes.

4. Remove meatballs to baking sheet and place in oven. Bake until meatballs are cooked through, about 15-18 minutes.

5. Slice dinner rolls in half and place a spoonful of salsa on each bottom slice. Top with meatballs and slices of cheese, onion, tomato, lettuce, and avocado.

PORK MEATBALL BÁNH MÌS

●●●

A bánh mì is a Vietnamese sub sandwich—and just like with American subs, there is a version with meatballs! The all-pork meatballs here are flavored with traditional Vietnamese ingredients, including fish sauce, which adds a distinct salty taste you may recognize from Asian dipping sauces and dishes. You can find fish sauce in Asian markets and in the ethnic aisle of your grocery store.

1 small cucumber, seeded and peeled
1 medium carrot, peeled
1 tablespoon salt
3 tablespoons sugar
1 pound ground pork
2 garlic cloves, minced
1 tablespoon fresh ginger, minced
¼ cup panko breadcrumbs
1 tablespoon soy sauce
1 tablespoon fish sauce
2 tablespoons fresh cilantro leaves, chopped
1 tablespoon vegetable or olive oil
4 hard sub rolls
Mayonnaise, for garnish

1. Using a vegetable peeler, cut cucumber and carrot into long shreds. Place vegetable peels in colander over a bowl and sprinkle with salt and sugar.

2. Loosely mix together pork, garlic, ginger, panko breadcrumbs, soy sauce, fish sauce, and cilantro. Shape into balls about 1½ inches in diameter.

3. Heat oil over medium-high heat, then add meatballs (in batches if necessary), turning two or three times during cooking time, until browned, about 6-8 minutes.

4. Turn heat down to medium and continue to turn while cooking until cooked through, about 12-15 minutes. Drain on a paper towel.

5. Add meatballs to rolls and top with cucumber and carrot. Garnish with mayonnaise and additional cilantro, if desired.

LAMB MEATBALL SUBS
with PICKLED ONION

●●●

Lamb is an intensely flavored meat, and these subs do the job of adding even more piquancy while still allowing the lamb to steal the show. These flavorful subs combine the pickled veggies of bánh mìs and the tomato-based sauce of Italian meatball subs, with distinctive Middle Eastern spices thrown in.

SANDWICHES

¾ cup white vinegar
3 tablespoons sugar
⅛ teaspoon salt
⅛ teaspoon ground cloves

1 medium onion, thinly sliced
6 hard sub rolls
¼ cup (½ stick) butter, softened

MEATBALLS

2 pounds ground lamb
3 garlic cloves, minced
¾ cup breadcrumbs
½ cup zinfandel or other full-bodied red wine
1 egg, lightly beaten

1 cup feta cheese, crumbled
1 teaspoon dried rosemary
¼ teaspoon curry powder
2 teaspoons salt
1 teaspoon black pepper

SAUCE

1 (28 ounce) can crushed tomatoes
1 bay leaf

1 teaspoon ground cumin
¼ teaspoon ground cinnamon
⅛ teaspoon ground cloves

1. In a small saucepan, bring vinegar, sugar, salt, and cloves to a boil over medium-high heat. Add onions and simmer until they are tender, about 1 minute. Remove from heat and let cool, then pour into a bowl and refrigerate, covered, for at least 15-20 minutes.

2. Loosely mix together lamb, garlic, breadcrumbs, wine, egg, feta cheese, rosemary, curry powder, salt, and pepper. Shape into balls about 2 inches in diameter.

3. In large saucepan, heat oil over medium-high heat. Add meatballs (in batches if necessary), turning two or three times during cooking time, until browned, but not cooked through, about 6-8 minutes.

4. Add tomatoes, bay leaf, cumin, cinnamon, and cloves. If meatballs were cooked in batches, add back in all meatballs.

5. Reduce heat to medium and simmer, covered, until meatballs are cooked through, about 15 minutes.

6. Remove meatballs with a slotted spoon and add, with some sauce, to rolls. Top with pickled onion.

FALAFEL SANDWICHES

● ● ●

Falafel is a popular street food in the city, but perhaps you didn't know how easy it is to make your own at home. All you need are some chickpeas and a food processor! This recipe is a little more complicated than that, of course, but it does produce deliciously simple vegetarian falafel that are perfect on top of pitas.

FALAFEL

1 (15 ounce) can chickpeas (garbanzo beans)
1 small garlic clove, roughly chopped
1 tablespoon minced onion
1 teaspoon lemon juice
¼ cup fresh parsley, chopped
1 teaspoon ground cumin
½ teaspoon baking soda
1 teaspoon salt
½ teaspoon black pepper
2 tablespoons olive oil

SANDWICHES

5 pitas
½ of 1 (7 ounce) container of hummus
Roasted red peppers, onion, tomato, and lettuce for garnish (optional)

1. Preheat oven to 375°F.

2. To food processor, add chickpeas, garlic, onion, lemon juice, parsley, cumin, baking soda, salt, and pepper. Pulse until minced but not pureed, scraping down the sides between pulses if necessary. Add a spoonful of water if mixture is too dry. Shape mixture into balls about 1½ inches in diameter.

3. Brush falafel with olive oil on all sides and place on a baking sheet. Bake until golden brown, about 20-25 minutes.

4. To warm pitas, place them in the oven for the last minute of baking time. Fill pitas with hummus and falafel. Garnish with roasted red peppers, onions, tomato, or lettuce if desired.

MIX 'N' MATCH

Try spreading some of the Tzatziki Sauce from page 37 on these Falafel Sandwiches!

Dinner
FAVORITES

CLASSIC ITALIAN MEATBALLS

●●●

Instead of being baked or fried, these meatballs are braised in tomato sauce, which infuses them with a hearty flavor. They're perfect for the quintessential Italian-American dish, spaghetti with meatballs.

MEATBALLS

1 pound ground beef
1 pound ground pork
1 pound ground veal
3 garlic cloves, minced
¼ cup grated Parmesan cheese
¼ cup breadcrumbs
2 large eggs, lightly beaten

2 tablespoons milk
1½ teaspoons fresh basil, chopped
1½ teaspoons fresh parsley, chopped
1 tablespoon salt
2 teaspoons black pepper

MARINARA SAUCE

2 tablespoons olive oil
1 small onion, finely chopped
2 cloves crushed garlic
2 (28 ounce) cans crushed tomatoes
2 (6 ounce) cans tomato paste

6 cups water
2 bay leaves
1½ teaspoons dried basil
½ teaspoon crushed red pepper
1½ teaspoons fresh parsley, chopped

1. Heat oil over medium-high heat. Add onion and cook, stirring occasionally, until it starts to soften, about 3-5 minutes. Add garlic and cook until onion is translucent, about 2 minutes more.

2. Reduce heat to low. Add tomatoes and cook for 20 minutes, stirring occasionally.

3. Add tomato paste and stir to combine. Then add water, bay leaves, basil, and crushed red pepper. Bring to boil on medium-high heat, then reduce heat to low and simmer 20 minutes.

4. Meanwhile, loosely mix together beef, pork, veal, garlic, Parmesan cheese, breadcrumbs, eggs, milk, basil, parsley, salt, and pepper. Shape into balls about 2-2½ inches in diameter.

5. Heat oil in skillet over medium-high heat, then add meatballs (in batches if necessary), turning during cooking time, until browned but not cooked through, about 6-8 minutes.

6. Add meatballs to sauce and simmer until cooked through, about 20 minutes. Serve over pasta.

EASY SLOW COOKER SPAGHETTI and MEATBALLS

●●●

This simplified version of spaghetti and meatballs uses pre-pared spaghetti sauce, dried herbs, and best of all, a slow cooker! Set it and forget it during your day, then have a family-friendly dinner waiting when you get home.

> 1 pound ground beef
> 1 pound bulk sweet Italian sausage
> ¼ cup shredded Parmesan cheese
> 1¼ cups Italian-seasoned breadcrumbs
> 2 large eggs, lightly beaten
> ½ cup milk
> 1 teaspoon garlic powder
> 1 teaspoon dried oregano or basil
> 2 teaspoons salt
> 1 teaspoon black pepper
> 6 cups spaghetti sauce

1. Loosely mix together beef, sausage, Parmesan cheese, breadcrumbs, eggs, milk, garlic powder, oregano or basil, salt, and pepper. Shape into balls about 2 inches in diameter.

2. Heat oil in skillet over medium-high heat, then add meat-balls (in batches if necessary), turning during cooking time, until browned but not cooked through, about 3-5 minutes.

3. Place meatballs in a 6-quart slow cooker. Pour spaghetti sauce on top. Cover and cook on low until meatballs are cooked through, about 4-5 hours. Serve over spaghetti noodles.

MIX 'N' MATCH

If you don't have a favorite homemade or jarred spaghetti sauce, use the Marinara Sauce recipe on page 80.

PESTO MEATBALLS with PINE NUTS

● ● ●

This pasta dish with turkey meatballs is light, palate-pleasing, and perfect for summer. The secret is using a high-quality extra-virgin olive oil, which will make sure your sauce doesn't taste heavy. Using fresh tomatoes at the peak of the season will make it even better!

MEATBALLS

2 pounds ground turkey (light and dark mix)
1 (8 ounce) container refrigerated pesto
1 cup breadcrumbs
½ cup pine nuts, toasted
1 teaspoon salt
½ teaspoon black pepper
1 tablespoon vegetable or olive oil

PASTA

1 (1 pint) carton grape or cherry tomatoes, halved
1–2 cherry peppers, chopped
1½ (16 ounce) packages pasta noodles, cooked
2–4 tablespoons high-quality extra-virgin olive oil
½ cup mozzarella cheese, shredded

1. Loosely mix together turkey, pesto, breadcrumbs, pine nuts, salt, and pepper. Shape into balls about 1 inch in diameter.

2. Heat oil in skillet over medium-high heat, then add meatballs (in batches if necessary), turning during cooking time, until browned but not cooked through, about 3-5 minutes. Remove meatballs to baking sheets.

3. Add tomatoes and cherry peppers to baking sheets, interspersed with meatballs. Cook until tomatoes are blistered, cherry peppers are tender, and meatballs are cooked through, about 10 minutes.

4. Toss hot pasta with olive oil and top with meatballs, tomatoes, and mozzarella cheese.

SPICY RED PEPPER MEATBALLS

● ● ●

The spice in these zesty meatballs comes from andouille sausage. Just remove the casings and you have pre-spiced pork to mix with your ground beef! A roasted red pepper adds more flavor, and cooked rice gives these meatballs a unique texture.

> ½ pound ground beef
> ½ pound andouille sausage, casings removed
> 2 garlic cloves, minced
> 2 tablespoons breadcrumbs
> ¼ cup rice, cooked
> 1 roasted red pepper (from jar), diced
> 1 large egg, lightly beaten
> 1 teaspoon salt
> ½ teaspoon black pepper
> 1 tablespoon olive oil

1. Loosely mix together beef, Andouille sausage, garlic, breadcrumbs, rice, roasted red pepper, egg, salt, and pepper. Shape into balls about 1½ inches in diameter.

2. Heat saucepan over medium-high heat, then add meatballs, turning two or three times, until browned, but not cooked through, about 6-8 minutes.

3. Turn heat down to medium and continue to turn while cooking until cooked through, about 10 minutes.

4. Remove from heat and drain on paper towels.

MIX 'N' MATCH

These meatballs are perfect with a Marinara Sauce like the one on page 80, or can be served in a soup like the Italian Wedding Soup on page 52.

MEATBALLS in RED WINE SAUCE

● ● ●

These meatballs are fit for a king—or just anybody who wants a filling meal that will make them feel like royalty! Make sure to serve them and their flavorful red wine sauce with crusty bread for dipping.

MEATBALLS

½ cup breadcrumbs

3 tablespoons milk (preferably whole)

¾ pound ground beef

½ pound ground pork

1 large egg, lightly beaten

2 teaspoons dried parsley

1 teaspoon crushed red pepper

1½ tablespoons olive oil, divided

½ cup ricotta cheese, drained

1 teaspoon salt

½ teaspoon black pepper

RED WINE SAUCE

1 medium onion, diced

3 garlic cloves, diced

2 tablespoons tomato paste

1 cup Chianti or other dry red wine

½ cup beef stock

1 (14.5 ounce) can tomato sauce

1. Preheat oven to 475°F.

2. Combine breadcrumbs and milk and let sit until breadcrumbs are saturated. Then add beef, pork, egg, parsley, crushed red pepper, ½ tablespoon of olive oil, ricotta cheese, salt, and pepper and loosely mix. Shape into balls about 2 inches in diameter.

3. Heat remaining olive oil in skillet over medium-high heat, then add meatballs (in batches if necessary), turning during cooking time, until browned but not cooked through, about 6-8 minutes.

4. Remove meatballs to baking sheet and place in oven. Bake until meatballs are cooked through, about 15 minutes.

5. Meanwhile, add onion and garlic to hot oil and cook, stirring occasionally, until soft, about 6 minutes.

6. Add tomato paste and stir until it coats onion and garlic, about 1 minute. Add wine and simmer, stirring occasionally, until reduced by half, about 5 minutes. Reduce heat to medium-low and add beef stock and tomato sauce. Add meatballs and cook for an additional 10 minutes. Serve over pasta and with some crusty bread.

VEAL MEATBALLS
with GRAVY

●●●

These decadent veal meatballs topped with elegant beef gravy are unrivaled as a special dinner treat. They're made differently from the usual meatballs, by combining cooked ground veal with mashed potatoes.

MEATBALLS

½ pound white potatoes, peeled and boiled

2 tablespoons vegetable oil

1 pound ground veal

1 garlic clove, minced

½ teaspoon fresh rosemary, chopped

2 teaspoons salt

1 teaspoon black pepper

3 slices white bread, crusts trimmed, torn into small pieces

½ cup milk

2 tablespoons fresh parsley, chopped

2 large eggs, lightly beaten, divided

¼ cup freshly grated Romano cheese

½ cup all-purpose flour

1 cup breadcrumbs

Oil for frying

TRADITIONAL GRAVY

2 tablespoons butter

1½ tablespoons flour

1 cup beef broth

1 teaspoon Worcestershire sauce

½ teaspoon dried thyme

½ teaspoon salt

¼ teaspoon black pepper

1. In a large skillet, heat oil over medium-high heat. Add veal, garlic, rosemary, salt and pepper. Cook, stirring occasionally and breaking up veal, until browned, about 8-10 minutes. Remove veal from skillet with slotted spoon and reserve fat in pan for gravy.

2. In small bowl, combine bread and milk until milk is absorbed. Set aside.

3. Mash potatoes with masher in large bowl. Then add veal, milk-bread mixture, parsley, 1 egg, and Romano cheese.

4. Shape into balls about 1 inch in diameter, then dip each ball into flour, then remaining egg, then breadcrumbs.

5. Heat oil in deep-fryer or in a large pot (about 2½ inches deep) on the stovetop to 350°F. Fry meatballs in batches until golden brown, about 4 minutes. Drain on paper towels and keep in a warmed oven while preparing gravy.

6. To make gravy, reheat pan drippings over medium heat and add butter. When butter is melted, add flour. Continue to heat, stirring constantly, until flour begins to brown, about 1-2 minutes. Add broth, Worcestershire sauce, thyme, salt, and black pepper.

7. Simmer over medium heat, stirring frequently, until gravy thickens, about 4-5 minutes. Spoon over meatballs.

SWEDISH MEATBALLS

● ● ●

Swedish meatballs are the only meatballs that come close to rivaling their Italian counterparts in popularity. Although their interior makeup is similar, Swedish meatballs are not always smothered in sauce, and are often eaten at room-temperature as a picnic food. Traditionally, they're served alongside ligonberry jam, which can be found online, in markets specializing in food from around the world, and yes, at IKEA, which made Swedish meatballs globally popular.

1 pound ground beef
1 pound ground pork
1 medium onion, finely chopped
½ cup breadcrumbs
1 tablespoon honey
¼ cup milk
1 large egg, lightly beaten
½ teaspoon ground nutmeg
2 teaspoons salt
1 teaspoon black pepper
1 tablespoon vegetable or olive oil
1 medium onion, finely chopped
Lingonberry jam, for serving

1. Loosely mix together beef, pork, onion, breadcrumbs, honey, milk, egg, nutmeg, salt, and pepper. Shape into balls about 1½ inches in diameter.

2. Heat saucepan over medium-high heat, then add meatballs, turning two or three times during cooking time, until browned, but not cooked through, about 6-8 minutes.

3. Turn heat down to medium and continue to turn while cooking until cooked through, about 10 minutes.

4. Remove from heat and drain on paper towels. Serve with lingonberry jam.

MIX 'N' MATCH

Swedish Meatballs are also often served topped with gravy, like the Traditional Gravy on page 90 or the Mushroom Sauce on page 116.

FRIED PORK MEATBALLS

● ● ●

Using a deep-fryer (or a pot of oil on the stove) means these meatballs couldn't be quicker to make! And because they're fried, they have a perfectly crispy outside. Just try to not pop one in your mouth until they've cooled!

1 pound ground pork
1 pound sweet Italian sausage, casings removed
½ cup breadcrumbs
¼ cup grated Parmesan cheese
2 egg yolks, lightly beaten
¼ cup milk
2 tablespoons fresh parsley, chopped
1 teaspoon lemon zest
2 teaspoons salt
1 teaspoon black pepper
Oil for frying

1. Loosely mix together pork, sausage, breadcrumbs, Parmesan cheese, egg yolks, milk, parsley, lemon zest, salt, and pepper. Shape into balls about 1½ inches in diameter.

2. Heat oil in deep-fryer or in a large pot (about 2½ inches deep) on the stovetop to about 350°F. Fry meatballs in batches until golden brown, about 3 minutes. Let drain on paper towels.

MIX 'N' MATCH

These meatballs go great with just about any sauce! Try them with the Barbecue Sauce on page 27 or the Cuban Black Bean Sauce on page 124.

TURKEY-SPINACH MEATBALLS

●●●

These healthy meatballs are packed with vitamins and nutrients—and they're tasty, too! In this unique recipe, the meatballs are browned under the broiler instead of in the pan. It requires a bit of skill to quickly pull them out, flip them, and put them back in, but the clean-up is a breeze!

1½ pounds ground turkey (light and dark mix)
1 (10 ounce) package frozen chopped spinach,
   thawed, drained, and squeezed in
   paper towels
2 garlic cloves, minced
½ cup breadcrumbs
½ cup grated Parmesan cheese
1 large egg, lightly beaten
2 tablespoons fresh parsley, chopped
1 teaspoon fennel seeds
1½ teaspoons salt
1 teaspoon black pepper
2 tablespoons olive oil
1 cup marinara sauce
¼ cup fresh basil, chopped, for garnish

1. Preheat broiler to 500°F.

2. Loosely mix together turkey, spinach, garlic, bread-crumbs, Parmesan cheese, egg, parsley, fennel, salt, and pepper. Shape into balls about 1 inch in diameter. Brush on all sides with olive oil and place on greased baking sheet.

3. Broil meatballs, turning often with tongs, until browned all over, about 6 minutes. Add marinara sauce and continue to broil until cooked through, an additional 10-12 minutes. Top with chopped basil and serve over pasta or rice.

MIX 'N' MATCH

If you don't have jarred or leftover sauce, use the Marinara Sauce recipe on page 80! You can also try them with the Spicy Dipping Sauce on page 24.

CHORIZO MEATBALLS with SALSA VERDE

●●●

If you've never tried salsa verde, you might be about to fall in love! It's made from tomatillos—green, husk-covered cousins of the tomato that can be found in your produce section.

SALSA VERDE

1 pound small and large tomatillos, husked, peeled, and halved

½ cup plus 1 tablespoon water, divided

1 tablespoon vegetable or olive oil

Skin of 1 medium onion

2 garlic cloves, minced

½ cup fresh cilantro, chopped

3 serrano chilies, ribs and seeds removed

1 teaspoon salt

MEATBALLS

1 pound ground beef

1 pound Mexican chorizo sausage, casings removed

1 medium onion, finely chopped

3 garlic cloves, minced

2 teaspoons ground cumin

1½ teaspoons dried oregano

½ cup breadcrumbs

1 large egg, lightly beaten

2 tablespoons milk

¼ cup Cheddar cheese, shredded

2 tablespoons fresh cilantro, chopped

2 teaspoons salt

1 teaspoon black pepper

1 tablespoon vegetable or olive oil

1. In food processor or blender, purée tomatillos and ½ cup water until smooth. Set aside.

2. In medium saucepan, heat oil over medium heat. Add onion peel and brown on one side, about 10-15 seconds. Flip with tongs and add garlic. Cook until tender, about 1 minute. Add tomatillos-water mixture and cook, stirring occasionally, until reduced slightly, about 15 minutes.

3. In food processor or blender, purée cilantro and chilies with 1 tablespoon water (add more if necessary). Add to saucepan with salt.

4. Cook, covered, stirring occasionally, until slightly lighter in color and further reduced, about 30 minutes. Remove onion skin before serving.

5. Meanwhile, preheat oven to 450°F.

6. Loosely mix together beef, chorizo, onion, garlic, cumin, oregano, breadcrumbs, egg, milk, Cheddar cheese, cilantro, salt, and pepper. Shape into balls about 2 inches in diameter.

7. Heat oil in skillet over medium-high heat, then add meatballs (in batches if necessary), turning during cooking time, until browned but not cooked through, about 6-8 minutes.

8. Remove meatballs to baking sheet and place in oven. Cook until meatballs are cooked through, about 15-18 minutes. Top with salsa verde and serve with rice.

CHEESY CHICKEN MEATBALLS

● ● ●

In this recipe, you'll brown the meatballs in the last step rather than the first, under the broiler. But before you do, top each meatball with some pizza sauce and a slice of mozzarella cheese—you'll love the result, which tastes like a mini chicken parm!

1¼ pounds ground chicken (light and dark mix)
1 small onion, finely chopped
1 garlic clove, minced
½ cup breadcrumbs
½ cup grated Romano cheese
1 large egg, lightly beaten
1½ teaspoons dried oregano
1 teaspoon salt
½ teaspoon black pepper
1 (14.5 ounce) can pizza sauce, divided
3 tablespoons olive oil
Approximately 12 slices mozzarella cheese

1. Preheat oven to 400°F.

2. Loosely mix together chicken, onion, garlic, breadcrumbs, Romano cheese, egg, oregano, salt, and pepper. Shape into balls about 2 inches in diameter. Place on baking sheet.

3. Mix together 1 tablespoon pizza sauce with olive oil. Brush onto top of meatballs. Bake for 15 minutes. Remove from oven and set oven to broil.

4. Spoon remaining pizza sauce over meatballs and top each one with a slice of mozzarella cheese.

5. Broil until cheese is bubbly and golden, about 3-5 minutes.

BUFFALO CHICKEN MEATBALLS

● ● ●

If you love buffalo wings, you'll love this meatball version, which is equally good as an appetizer or served over rice as a meal.

MEATBALLS

1¼ cups breadcrumbs, divided
1 teaspoon paprika
½ teaspoon cayenne pepper
1½ teaspoon black pepper, divided
1 pound ground chicken (light and dark mix)
½ pound turkey andouille sausage, casings removed
½ cup rice, cooked
2 garlic cloves, minced
1 tablespoon blue cheese dressing
2 large eggs, lightly beaten, divided
1 teaspoon salt
½ cup all-purpose flour
1 tablespoon vegetable or olive oil

BUFFALO SAUCE

3 tablespoons butter
1 small onion, finely chopped
3 garlic cloves, minced
1 (8 ounce) can tomato sauce
¼ cup chicken broth
2 tablespoons ketchup
1–2 tablespoons hot sauce (to taste)
2 teaspoons soy sauce
2 tablespoons brown sugar
1 teaspoon chili powder
¼ teaspoon cayenne pepper
½ teaspoon salt
1 teaspoon black pepper
1 tablespoon apple cider vinegar

1. Preheat oven to 450°F.

2. Mix together 1 cup breadcrumbs, paprika, cayenne pepper, and 1 teaspoon black pepper. Set aside.

3. Loosely mix together remaining ¼ cup breadcrumbs, chicken, sausage, rice, garlic, blue cheese dressing, ½ of beaten eggs, salt, and remaining ½ teaspoon pepper. Shape into balls about 2 inches in diameter. Roll each meatball in remaining egg, then flour, then breadcrumb mixture.

4. Heat oil in skillet over medium-high heat, then add meatballs (in batches if necessary), turning during cooking time, until browned but not cooked through, about 5-7 minutes.

5. Remove meatballs to baking sheet and place in oven. Cook until meatballs are cooked through, about 15-18 minutes.

6. Meanwhile, in medium saucepan, melt butter over medium-high heat. Add onion and garlic and cook until tender, about 3-5 minutes. Add remaining ingredients, except vinegar. Bring to a simmer, then reduce heat to low and cook, uncovered, until slightly thickened, about 15 minutes. Stir in vinegar. Pour over meatballs.

MEATBALL SHISH KEBABS

● ● ●

One of the easiest ways to prepare meatballs is by grilling them! These Middle Eastern-inspired meatballs are threaded onto skewers along with peppers and onions for a barbecue treat that's sure to be a big hit with your family and friends.

MEATBALLS

1 pound ground beef
1 pound ground turkey
2 garlic cloves, minced
¼ cup breadcrumbs
1 large egg, lightly beaten
1 tablespoon olive oil
1½ tablespoons ground coriander
2 teaspoons ground cumin
½ teaspoon ground nutmeg
1 teaspoon cayenne pepper
2 teaspoons salt
½ teaspoon black pepper

KEBABS

1 red bell pepper
1 green bell pepper
2 medium onions

1. Loosely mix together beef, turkey, garlic, breadcrumbs, egg, olive oil, coriander, cumin, nutmeg, cayenne pepper, salt, and pepper. Shape into balls about 1 inch in diameter.

2. Chop bell peppers and onions into pieces about 1 inch long and ½ inch wide. Thread onto skewers with meatballs.

3. Heat a grill pan or barbecue grill over medium heat, then grill the meatballs (working in batches if necessary), turning two or three times until brown all over and cooked through, about 6-8 minutes.

MIX 'N' MATCH

Try these meatballs instead of the lamb variety in the Meatball Subs with Pickled Onion on page 75!

MEDITERRANEAN PORK MEATBALLS

● ● ●

The chopped olives in these savory meatballs give them a delicious salty, yet almost fruity taste. But their real secret ingredient is cream cheese, which gives them a rich flavor and airy texture.

1 pound ground pork
1 pound bulk sausage, sweet or hot (to taste)
3 garlic cloves, minced
⅓ cup green olives, finely chopped
1 cup breadcrumbs
1 (8 ounce) package whipped cream cheese, softened
1 teaspoon dried thyme
1 large egg, lightly beaten
1 teaspoon black pepper
1 tablespoon vegetable or olive oil

1. Preheat oven to 450°F.

2. Mix together pork, sausage, garlic, olives, breadcrumbs, cream cheese, thyme, egg, and pepper until cream cheese is incorporated throughout. Shape into balls about 1½ inches in diameter.

3. Heat oil in skillet over medium-high heat, then add meatballs (in batches if necessary), turning during cooking time, until browned but not cooked through, about 6-8 minutes.

4. Remove meatballs to baking sheet and place in oven. Bake until meatballs are cooked through, about 15-18 minutes.

MIX 'N' MATCH

Try these meatballs with the Red Wine Sauce on page 89 or the Buffalo Sauce on page 102!

TURKEY MEATBALLS
with COUSCOUS

● ● ●

These veggie-filled meatballs are cooked in the oven to make the stovetop less chaotic while you're making the accompanying tomato sauce.

TOMATO SAUCE

2 tablespoons olive oil
1 medium onion, finely chopped
2 garlic cloves, finely chopped
1 (28 ounce can) crushed tomatoes
¼ cup orange juice
2 teaspoons orange zest
1 teaspoon dried rosemary

½ teaspoon dried thyme
½ teaspoon ground cumin
⅛ teaspoon cayenne pepper
⅛ teaspoon ground cinnamon
1 bay leaf
1½ teaspoons salt
1 teaspoon black pepper

MEATBALLS

1 pound ground turkey
  (light and dark mix)
2 garlic cloves, minced
1 medium carrot,
  peeled and grated
1 medium zucchini,
  peeled and grated
¼ cup couscous, cooked

2 tablespoons breadcrumbs
1 teaspoon paprika
2 tablespoons milk
1 large egg, lightly beaten
1 teaspoon salt
½ teaspoon black pepper
1 tablespoon vegetable
  or olive oil

1. Preheat oven to 450°F.

2. Heat oil over medium-high heat. Add onions and cook, stirring, for 2 minutes. Add garlic and continue to cook until onions are translucent and garlic is tender, about 2-3 minutes more.

3. Reduce heat to medium-low. Add tomatoes, orange juice, orange zest, rosemary, thyme, cumin, cayenne pepper, cinnamon, bay leaf, salt, and pepper. Simmer, uncovered, stirring occasionally, until reduced by a third, about 15 minutes. Remove bay leaf.

4. Meanwhile, loosely mix together turkey, garlic, carrot, zucchini, couscous, breadcrumbs, paprika, milk, egg, salt, and pepper. Shape into balls about 1½ inches in diameter.

5. In separate pan, heat oil over medium-high heat, then add meatballs (in batches if necessary), turning during cooking time, until browned but not cooked through, about 6-8 minutes.

6. Place meatballs in a single layer in a 13 x 9-inch pan. Pour sauce over meatballs and bake until meatballs are cooked through, about 15-18 minutes. Serve over additional couscous.

HAWAIIAN MEATBALLS

● ● ●

This popular homestyle meatball dish most likely didn't originate in the Aloha State, but is called Hawaiian Meatballs because of its sweet ingredient—pineapple. The pineapple juice is used to make the tangy sauce, and the pineapple chunks are added back in with chopped bell peppers at the end for even more sweet-yet-sour flavor.

MEATBALLS

1 pound ground beef
½ pound ground pork
1 small onion, finely chopped
¼ cup cracker crumbs
1 large egg, lightly beaten
1 teaspoon paprika
1 teaspoon salt
½ teaspoon black pepper
1 tablespoon vegetable or olive oil

HAWAIIAN SAUCE

1 (20 ounce) can pineapple chunks in juice
2½ tablespoons cornstarch
¼ cup brown sugar
2 tablespoons ketchup
3 tablespoons apple cider vinegar
2 tablespoons soy sauce
1 bell pepper, diced
Crushed red pepper, for garnish

1. Loosely mix together beef, pork, onion, cracker crumbs, egg, paprika, salt, and pepper. Shape into balls about 1 inch in diameter.

2. Heat oil in skillet over medium-high heat, then add meatballs, turning two or three times during cooking time, until browned, but not cooked through, about 6-8 minutes. Remove from heat and drain on paper towels. Set aside.

3. Drain juice from can of pineapples and set aside pineapple chunks.

4. Heat large saucepan over medium-low heat. Combine pineapple juice, cornstarch, brown sugar, ketchup, vinegar, and soy sauce. Cook, stirring constantly, until thickened, about 10-15 minutes.

5. Add meatballs, reserved pineapple chunks, and bell pepper. Bring to a simmer, then reduce heat to low, stirring occasionally, until peppers have just become tender, about 15 minutes. Top with crushed red pepper and serve over rice.

CHIPOTLE MEATBALL SKEWERS

● ● ●

Here's another great meatball recipe that features chipotle chilies, which you can find packed in small cans of adobo sauce at Mexican grocery stores and in the ethnic aisle of your supermarket. Thread vegetables like onions and peppers onto the skewers with the meatballs for even more flavor!

MEATBALLS

1½ pounds ground beef
1 small onion, finely chopped
2 garlic cloves, minced
¼ cup breadcrumbs
1 large egg, lightly beaten
1 tablespoon olive oil
¼ cup fresh cilantro, chopped
1 teaspoon ground cumin
1 chipotle chili (from can of chipotle chilies
   in adobo sauce), chopped
1½ teaspoons salt
1 teaspoon black pepper

SAUCE

1 (8 ounce) can tomato sauce
½ teaspoon adobo sauce from canned
   chipotle chilies
1 garlic clove, minced

1. Loosely mix together beef, onion, garlic, breadcrumbs, egg, olive oil, cilantro, cumin, chipotle chili, salt, and pepper. Shape into balls about 1 inch in diameter. Thread onto skewers.

2. In small saucepan over medium heat, combine tomato sauce, adobo sauce, and garlic and cook, stirring occasionally, until heated through, about 5 minutes.

3. Heat a grill pan or barbecue grill over medium heat, then grill the meatballs (working in batches if necessary), turning two or three times until brown all over, about 3-5 minutes. Using basting brush, cover with sauce and grill, turning, until meatballs are cooked through, about 2-4 minutes more. Serve with salsa or guacamole.

MIX 'N' MATCH

Try these meatballs with the Salsa Verde on page 98 or the Cuban Black Bean Sauce on page 124.

MEATBALLS in CREAMY CHEESE SAUCE

●●●

The decadent cheese sauce in this dish is a cross between mac and cheese and cheese fondue! That's why these meatballs are great over pasta or simply with fondue forks and crusty bread. Don't skip the mustard in the sauce, which (with its emulsifying properties) helps ensure the cheese doesn't break up while being melted.

MEATBALLS

1½ pounds ground beef
1 medium onion, finely chopped
2 garlic cloves, minced
1 cup quick-cooking oats
1 large egg, lightly beaten
½ cup milk

1 teaspoon Worcestershire sauce
2 teaspoons ground cumin
1½ teaspoons chili powder
1 teaspoon salt
½ teaspoon black pepper
1 tablespoon vegetable or olive oil

CHEESE SAUCE

3 cups sharp Cheddar cheese, shredded
1 cup Gruyere cheese, shredded
2 tablespoons cornstarch
1 tablespoon butter
2 garlic cloves, minced

1 (12 ounce) bottle light beer
¾ teaspoon Dijon mustard
½ teaspoon salt
½ teaspoon black pepper
¼–½ teaspoon (to taste) hot sauce

1. Loosely mix together beef, onion, garlic, oats, egg, milk, Worcestershire sauce, cumin, chili powder, salt, and pepper. Shape into balls about 1½ inches in diameter.

2. Heat oil over medium-high heat, then add meatballs (in batches if necessary), turning two or three times during cooking time, until browned, about 6-8 minutes.

3. Turn heat down to medium and continue to turn while cooking until cooked through, about 10 minutes. Drain on a paper towel and set aside, covered.

4. Toss together Cheddar cheese, Gruyere cheese, and cornstarch. Set aside.

5. In a large saucepan, melt butter over low heat. Add garlic and cook until soft but not brown, about 1 minute. Add beer, Dijon mustard, salt, and pepper. Cook, stirring occasionally, until warm, about 3-5 minutes.

6. Add Cheddar cheese mixture in batches and whisk continually until smooth. Stir in hot sauce and immediately remove from heat.

7. Add meatballs and completely cover in sauce; cover and let sit for 1-2 minutes to reheat meatballs.

MEATBALLS in MUSHROOM SAUCE

● ● ●

Experiment with different kinds of mushrooms in this piquant meatball sauce. A mixture works best, but you can use any kind you prefer, like cremini, button, oyster, portobello, or shiitake. Serve over potatoes—mashed or baked!

MEATBALLS

1 pound ground beef
1 pound ground veal
1 medium onion, finely chopped
½ cup panko breadcrumbs
1 large egg, lightly beaten

2 tablespoons soy sauce
½ teaspoon nutmeg
¼ teaspoon cinnamon
1 teaspoon black pepper

MUSHROOM SAUCE

3 tablespoons butter
1 pound mushrooms, such as
   cremini, oyster, or shiitake,
   stemmed and sliced
3 garlic cloves, minced
⅓ cup all-purpose flour
4 cups beef broth

1 tablespoon balsamic vinegar
¾ cup sour cream
1 teaspoon salt
1 teaspoon black pepper
2 tablespoons fresh parsley,
   chopped, for garnish

1. Loosely mix together beef, veal, onion, panko breadcrumbs, egg, soy sauce, nutmeg, cinnamon, and pepper. Shape into balls about 1½ inches in diameter.

2. Heat saucepan over medium-high heat, then add meatballs, turning two or three times during cooking time, until browned, but not cooked through, about 6-8 minutes. Remove from heat and drain on paper towels.

3. Drain all but 1 tablespoon fat from pan. Add butter and melt, then add mushrooms and cook, stirring frequently, until mushrooms begin to brown, about 3-5 minutes. Add garlic and stir until garlic is tender but not browned, about 1 minute.

4. Add flour and whisk constantly until flour is absorbed and starts to brown, about 1 minute.

5. Gradually add in beef broth and cook, whisking constantly, until slightly thickened, about 1-2 minutes. Reduce heat to low and add balsamic vinegar, sour cream, salt, and pepper.

6. Stir in meatballs and cook, stirring occasionally, until heated through and thickened, about 8-10 minutes. Add more sour cream or broth to adjust consistency. Garnish with parsley.

SWEET and SOUR MEATBALLS

● ● ●

Though they have some Asian flavors, these meatballs are distinctly American, and they have a distinctly American ingredient—a packet of French onion soup and dip mix. You'll love the way it tastes both in the sauce and in the meatballs themselves!

MEATBALLS

1 pound ground beef
1 pound ground pork
1 medium onion, finely chopped
2 garlic cloves, minced
½ cup breadcrumbs
1 large egg, lightly beaten

½ of 1 (2 ounce) envelope dry French onion soup and dip mix
1 teaspoon dried parsley
½ teaspoon salt
½ teaspoon black pepper
1 tablespoon vegetable or olive oil

SWEET AND SOUR SAUCE

1 cup ketchup
1 cup apple cider vinegar
½ cup water
½ cup orange juice
2 tablespoons soy sauce
½ cup sugar
½ of 1 (2 ounce) envelope dry French onion soup and dip mix
1 cup golden raisins

1. Loosely mix together beef, pork, onion, garlic, breadcrumbs, egg, French onion soup mix, parsley, salt, and pepper. Shape into balls about 1½ inches in diameter.

2. Heat oil over medium-high heat, then add meatballs (in batches if necessary), turning two or three times during cooking time, until browned, about 6-8 minutes. Remove from heat and drain on paper towels. Set aside.

3. Heat large saucepan over medium-low heat. Combine ketchup, apple cider vinegar, water, orange juice, soy sauce, sugar, French onion soup mix, and raisins. Cook, stirring constantly, until heated through and slightly thickened, about 10-15 minutes.

4. Add meatballs and bring to a simmer, then reduce heat to medium-low, stirring occasionally, until meatballs are cooked through. Serve over rice or egg noodles.

KATLETI MEATBALLS

● ● ●

Meatballs are a comfort food all over the world—and Russia is no exception. These *Katleti* (Russian for "meat cutlets") contain a spoonful of mayonnaise to give them a depth of flavor and help keep the balls together.

> 1 pound ground pork
> 1 pound ground turkey
> 1 medium onion, finely chopped
> 2 garlic cloves, minced
> 2 slices white bread, crusts trimmed,
>   torn into small pieces
> 1 tablespoon mayonnaise
> 3 tablespoons fresh parsley, chopped
> 2 teaspoons salt
> 1 teaspoon black pepper
> 1 tablespoon vegetable or olive oil

1. Preheat oven to 450°F.

2. Loosely mix together pork, turkey, onion, garlic, bread, mayonnaise, parsley, salt, and pepper. Shape into balls about 1½ inches in diameter.

3. Heat oil in skillet over medium-high heat, then add meatballs (in batches if necessary), turning during cooking time, until browned but not cooked through, about 6-8 minutes.

4. Remove meatballs to baking sheet and place in oven. Cook until meatballs are cooked through, about 12-15 minutes.

MIX 'N' MATCH

These versatile meatballs are delicious with just about any sauce! Try them with the the Mushroom Sauce on page 116 or the Barbecue Sauce on page 27.

Extraordinary
MEATBALLS

MEATBALLS with CUBAN BLACK BEAN SAUCE

● ● ●

The genius behind the Cuban Black Bean Sauce paired with these meatballs is that it doubles as a side. Traditionally, the sauce is served cold, but it's just as delicious warm.

MEATBALLS

1¼ cups breadcrumbs, divided
1 teaspoon garlic powder
1 teaspoon black pepper
1 pound ground beef
½ pound ground pork
1 medium onion, finely chopped
1 small jalapeño pepper, finely chopped

1 teaspoon dried thyme
1 teaspoon chili powder
2 large eggs, lightly beaten, divided
1 teaspoon salt
½ cup all-purpose flour
1 tablespoon vegetable or olive oil

BLACK BEAN SAUCE

1 (15 ounce) can black beans, rinsed and drained
1 red bell pepper, finely chopped
1 small onion, finely chopped
½ cup orange juice

2 tablespoons balsamic vinegar
2 garlic cloves, minced
¼ teaspoon salt
¼ teaspoon black pepper

1. Preheat oven to 450°F.

2. Mix together 1 cup breadcrumbs, garlic powder, and pepper. Set aside.

3. Loosely mix together remaining ¼ cup breadcrumbs, beef, pork, onion, thyme, chili powder, half of beaten eggs, and salt. Shape into balls about 1 inch in diameter. Roll each meatball in remaining egg, then flour, then breadcrumb mixture.

4. Heat oil in skillet over medium-high heat, then add meatballs (in batches if necessary), turning two or three times during cooking time, until browned but not cooked through, about 5-7 minutes.

5. Remove meatballs to baking sheet and place in oven. Bake until meatballs are cooked through, about 15-18 minutes.

6. Meanwhile, in medium bowl, mash black beans with potato masher or fork.

7. Add bell pepper, onion, orange juice, balsamic vinegar, garlic, salt, and pepper and mix until combined.

8. Chill the sauce until ready to serve, or, if desired, heat before serving with meatballs and rice.

MOROCCAN LAMB MEATBALLS

●●●

If you were making meatballs in Morocco, the first thing you'd reach for is your tagine. If you don't happen to have this North African clay pot, however, you can easily make do with a large skillet that has a lid (or just a makeshift lid of a pie plate or pizza pan).

1 lemon
1 pound ground lamb
3 medium onions, finely chopped, divided
1 tablespoon fresh cilantro, chopped
1 teaspoon ground cumin
1 teaspoon cinnamon
2 teaspoons salt, divided
½ teaspoon black pepper
2 tablespoons olive oil
1 small red bell pepper, chopped
½ serrano chili, seeded and finely chopped
1 teaspoon fresh ginger, minced
2 medium white potatoes, peeled
  and cut into wedges
1 cup lamb or beef stock
1 tablespoon tomato paste
¼ teaspoon turmeric
⅛ teaspoon saffron (optional)

1. Zest and juice lemon and set aside juice.

2. Loosely mix together lemon zest, lamb, 1 onion, cilantro, cumin, cinnamon, half of salt, and pepper. Shape into balls about 1½ inches in diameter.

3. Heat oil over medium-high heat in tagine or large skillet with lid. Add remaining onions, bell pepper, and serrano chili and cook until they start to become tender, about 3-5 minutes. Add ginger and cook 1 minute more.

4. Add potatoes, reserved lemon juice, lamb or beef stock, tomato paste, turmeric, saffron, and remaining salt. Add meatballs, then reduce heat to medium-low and cook, covered, stirring and turning meatballs occasionally, until liquid has reduced and potatoes and meatballs are cooked through, about 30-40 minutes. Serve over rice or couscous.

DANISH MEATBALLS
with DILL SAUCE

●●●

Like many ethnic American recipes, this one is inspired by Danish flavors, rather than being a traditional Danish preparation. Traditionally, Danish meatballs (called *frikadeller*) are a picnic food, served cold alongside vegetables and coleslaw. In this dish, however, the *frikadeller* are warm and smothered in a creamy sauce made from dill, an herb commonly found in Danish food.

MEATBALLS

1 pound ground veal
1 pound ground pork
1 medium onion, finely chopped
2 garlic cloves, minced
½ cup breadcrumbs
2 large eggs, lightly beaten
½ cup half-and-half
2 teaspoons salt
1 teaspoon black pepper

DILL SAUCE

½ cup (1 stick) butter
¼ cup all-purpose flour
2 cups chicken broth
¼ cup fresh dill, chopped
1 (16 ounce) carton sour cream
1 teaspoon salt
½ teaspoon black pepper

1. Preheat oven to 450°F.

2. Loosely mix together veal, pork, onion, garlic, breadcrumbs, eggs, half-and-half, salt, and pepper. Shape into balls about 1½ inches in diameter.

3. Heat oil in skillet over medium-high heat, then add meatballs (in batches if necessary), turning two or three times during cooking time, until browned but not cooked through, about 6-8 minutes.

4. Remove meatballs to baking sheet and place in oven. Bake until meatballs are cooked through, about 12-15 minutes.

5. Meanwhile, melt the butter in a large saucepan over medium-high heat. Add flour and whisk until incorporated, then add chicken broth. Reduce heat to low and cook, stirring constantly, until sauce starts to thicken, about 8-10 minutes. Stir in dill, sour cream, salt, and pepper.

6. Pour sauce over meatballs and serve with rice or potatoes.

XIU MAI (VIETNAMESE MEATBALLS)

● ● ●

Xiu Mai are all-pork meatballs, traditionally served during dim sum—a sort of Sunday brunch of tiny appetizers popular in Vietnam and other Asian countries. This recipe uses fish sauce, which can be found in Asian grocery stores and in the ethnic aisle of your supermarket. It will give the dish a certain *je ne sais quoi* that's missing otherwise, but only you will know if you cheat and just add a bit extra soy sauce instead!

MEATBALLS

2 pounds ground pork
3 garlic cloves, minced
2 shallots, finely chopped
1 (8 ounce) can water chestnuts, finely chopped
1 large egg, lightly beaten
1 tablespoon fish sauce
1 teaspoon soy sauce
1 teaspoon black pepper
1 tablespoon vegetable or olive oil

TOMATO SAUCE

1 tablespoon vegetable or olive oil
3 garlic cloves, finely chopped
3 tablespoons tomato paste
1 (14.5 ounce) can crushed tomatoes
1 cup water
2 teaspoons soy sauce
1 tablespoon fish sauce
1 tablespoon sugar
¼ cup fresh cilantro leaves, as garnish

1. Loosely mix together pork, garlic, shallots, water chestnuts, egg, fish sauce, soy sauce, and pepper. Shape into balls about 1½ inches in diameter.

2. Heat oil in skillet over medium-high heat, then add meatballs (in batches if necessary), turning two or three times during cooking time, until browned but not cooked through, about 6-8 minutes. Remove meatballs with slotted spoon and drain on paper towels.

3. Add garlic and cook, stirring, until it starts to soften, about 1 minute. Add tomato paste, crushed tomatoes, water, soy sauce, fish sauce, and sugar.

4. Bring to a simmer, then reduce heat to medium-low and add meatballs back in. Cook, stirring occasionally, until sauce is reduced slightly and meatballs are cooked through, about 20-25 minutes. Garnish with cilantro and serve with rice.

INDIAN MEATBALLS in CURRY SAUCE

● ● ●

This fragrant dish mixes Indian-spiced meatballs with a coconut milk-based curry. It's perfect for mixing up your meatball repertoire! Coconut milk (not to be confused with coconut water) is sold in a can, often in the Asian or ethnic aisle. It gives this dish a delicious buttery texture without the calories of a usual cream sauce.

MEATBALLS

1 pound ground lamb
½ pound ground turkey
2 garlic cloves, minced
1 teaspoon fresh ginger, minced
½ teaspoon ground cumin
¼ teaspoon paprika

⅛ teaspoon turmeric
1 large egg, lightly beaten
1 teaspoon salt
¼ teaspoon black pepper
1 tablespoon vegetable
  or olive oil

CURRY SAUCE

2 tablespoons vegetable oil
6 medium shallots, chopped
5 garlic cloves, minced
1 teaspoon fresh ginger, minced
2 medium tomatoes, chopped
½ cup water
1 (14 ounce) can unsweetened
  full-fat coconut milk

1 teaspoon curry powder
½ teaspoon ground cumin
½ teaspoon ground coriander
½ teaspoon cayenne pepper
½ teaspoon salt
¼ teaspoon black pepper
1 tablespoon lemon juice

1. Loosely mix together lamb, turkey, garlic, ginger, cumin, paprika, turmeric, egg, salt, and pepper. Shape into balls about 1½ inches in diameter.

2. Heat oil in skillet over medium-high heat, then add meatballs (in batches if necessary), turning two or three times during cooking time, until browned, about 6-8 minutes. Remove from heat and drain on paper towels. Set aside.

3. Meanwhile, heat oil for curry sauce in large saucepan over medium-low heat. Add shallots and cook until they start to turn translucent, about 3-5 minutes. Add garlic and ginger and cook 1 minute more. Add tomatoes, water, coconut milk, curry powder, cumin, coriander, cayenne pepper, salt, and pepper. Bring to a simmer, then reduce heat to low.

4. Add meatballs and cook, stirring occasionally, until meatballs are cooked through and sauce is slightly reduced, about 15-20 minutes. Stir in lemon juice. Serve over rice.

CHICKEN CURRY RICE BALLS

●●●

Unlike the Italian rice balls in the Appetizers chapter, these Asian rice balls use sushi rice. If you've ever had a sushi roll, you know the rice is super-sticky. In order to keep it from sticking to your fingers, use waxed paper to flatten out the balls you've made, then reform them around the chicken curry. Pass these rice balls out at a party and they're sure to impress.

1 tablespoon vegetable or olive oil
½ pound chicken sausage, casings removed
1 medium shallot, finely chopped
1 garlic clove, minced
2 scallions, finely chopped
½ teaspoon salt
¼ teaspoon black pepper
3 cups cooked sushi rice
1-3 tablespoons hot water (if needed)
1 cup all-purpose flour
1 large egg, beaten
1 cup panko breadcrumbs
Oil for frying

1. Heat oil in skillet over medium heat, then add chicken sausage, shallot, and garlic. Cook, stirring frequently and breaking up meat, until cooked through, about 8-10 minutes. Drain off fat. Stir in scallions, salt, and pepper.

2. If rice is dry and not sticking together, add hot water gradually until it becomes sticky.

3. Shape rice into balls about 1 inch in diameter. Then, one by one, place rice ball in between two small pieces of waxed paper. Press down on waxed paper to flatten ball. Remove top sheet of waxed paper.

4. Place approximately ¾ tablespoon chicken sausage mixture in the center of each ball. Lift up each corner of waxed paper in order to bring rice up around the filling. Press together to seal tightly.

5. Dip each ball into flour, then eggs, then breadcrumbs.

6. Heat oil in deep-fryer or in a large pot (about 2 inches deep) on the stovetop to 350°F. Fry rice balls in batches until golden brown, about 1-2 minutes. Let drain on paper towels.

MIX 'N' MATCH

Try dipping these rice balls in the Spicy Dipping Sauce on page 24!

PAN-FRIED SALMON BALLS

● ● ●

Thanks to how easily salmon flakes, these tasty fish balls are a cinch to make. Use inexpensive canned salmon, or make them downright gourmet by using fresh or even wild salmon. Make sure to try them with tartar sauce!

2 pounds canned salmon or fresh salmon,
    cooked, skinned, deboned,
    and flaked with a fork
¼ cup oyster sauce
1 tablespoon soy sauce
1 tablespoon mayonnaise
2 large eggs, lightly beaten
4 scallions, finely chopped
1½ tablespoons fresh ginger, minced
3 garlic cloves, minced
2 cups panko breadcrumbs
½ teaspoon crushed red pepper
¼ teaspoon black pepper
2 tablespoons vegetable or olive oil
Tartar sauce, for serving

1. Loosely mix together salmon, oyster sauce, soy sauce, mayonnaise, egg, scallions, ginger, garlic, breadcrumbs, crushed red pepper, and black pepper. Shape into balls about 1 inch in diameter.

2. Heat oil in large skillet over medium heat, then add salmon balls (in batches if necessary), turning two or three times during cooking time, until cooked through and slightly browned, about 10-15 minutes. Remove from heat and drain on paper towels. Serve with tartar sauce.

MIX 'N' MATCH

Instead of tartar sauce, try dipping these salmon balls into the Ginger-Soy Sauce on page 139!

SHRIMP BALLS with GINGER-SOY SAUCE

● ● ●

These shrimp balls are a bit time-consuming, but they're so much fun! For best results, use raw shrimp, making sure to peel and devein them first. Give them a fresh boost by tossing them with a spoonful of salt, letting sit for a few minutes, then rinsing with cool water and patting dry with paper towels before adding to the food processor.

SHRIMP BALLS

1 pound raw shrimp, peeled, deveined, and roughly chopped
1 large egg
¾ teaspoon toasted sesame oil
2 teaspoons olive oil
¼ teaspoon soy sauce
1 tablespoon cornstarch
1 teaspoon sugar
½ teaspoon salt
⅛ teaspoon black pepper
1 tablespoon scallion, finely chopped
20-24 refrigerated wonton skins or 10-12 egg roll wrappers
Oil for frying

GINGER-SOY SAUCE

¼ cup soy sauce
3 tablespoons rice vinegar
¼ teaspoon toasted sesame oil
1 tablespoon fresh ginger, minced
2 teaspoons sugar

1. In food processor, combine shrimp, egg, sesame oil, olive oil, soy sauce, cornstarch, sugar, salt, and pepper. Grind until it's the consistency of a paste, pausing to scrape down sides as necessary. Transfer to a bowl.

2. Add scallions and stir to combine. Cover and refrigerate for 30 minutes, or up to 1 hour. Then shape mixture into balls, each about ½ inch in diameter.

3. With a pizza cutter or knife, cut wonton skins or egg roll wrappers into ribbons, as thin as possible. Place into a pile on a plate or cutting board.

4. Roll each shrimp ball in ribbons and set aside.

5. Heat oil in deep-fryer or in a large pot (about 2 inches deep) on the stovetop to 350°F. Fry shrimp balls in batches until golden brown, about 1-2 minutes. Let drain on paper towels.

6. To make ginger-soy sauce, combine soy sauce, rice vinegar, sesame oil, ginger, and sugar and mix until sugar is dissolved. Serve with shrimp balls.

CHICKEN KEBABS

●●●

On-the-go and hungry in India? You just might turn to a street-side snack of a kebab, or meat skewer. These chicken meatballs are actually ovals, and are formed around the skewers themselves, then dusted with spices just before grilling. If you have trouble getting the meat mixture to stick on the skewer, try refrigerating it for a few hours beforehand.

1 teaspoon paprika
½ teaspoon ground coriander
½ teaspoon ground cumin
½ teaspoon dried oregano
½ teaspoon ground cardamom
¼ teaspoon fennel seed
¼ teaspoon black pepper
1 pound ground chicken
½ pound turkey andouille sausage,
    casings removed
2 garlic cloves, minced
1 tablespoon fresh ginger, minced
2 tablespoons mayonnaise
1 large egg, lightly beaten
1½ teaspoons salt
Juice from 1 lime

1. In small bowl, mix together paprika, coriander, cumin, oregano, cardamom, fennel seed, and black pepper. Set aside.

2. Loosely mix together chicken, turkey sausage, garlic, ginger, mayonnaise, egg, salt, and half of spice mixture.

3. Form into elongated meatballs by shaping the mixture into a 2-inch oval around the pointy end of each skewer. Sprinkle remaining spice mixture on each side of kebab and pat to work into meat slightly.

4. Heat an oiled grill pan or barbecue grill over high heat, then grill the kebabs (working in batches if necessary), turning two or three times until brown all over and cooked through, about 5-7 minutes. Drizzle with lime juice.

MIX 'N' MATCH

These chicken kebabs are fantastic when paired with the Tzatziki Sauce on page 37!

ZUCCHINI-WRAPPED MEATBALLS

● ● ●

An elegant appetizer or an incredibly original main course, these delightful meatballs get a special sweet-and-spicy flavor from hoisin sauce, a dipping sauce that can be found at Asian grocery stores or in the ethnic aisle of supermarkets. If you can't find it, simply substitute ¼ cup barbecue sauce mixed with ¼ cup soy sauce.

> 3 medium zucchinis
> 1 pound ground turkey
> ¾ cup panko breadcrumbs
> 1 medium onion, finely chopped
> 1 garlic clove, minced
> 1 teaspoon dried basil
> 1 large egg, lightly beaten
> ¼ teaspoon red pepper flakes
> 1 tablespoon soy sauce
> ¼ teaspoon salt
> ¼ teaspoon black pepper
> 1 tablespoon vegetable or olive oil
> ½ cup hoisin sauce

1. Preheat oven to 350°F.

2. Using a sharp vegetable peeler, slice zucchini lengthwise into wide, flat ribbons. Add to boiling water in medium saucepan and cook until firm yet tender, about 2 minutes. Immediately drain and rinse with cold water. Dry on paper towels.

3. Loosely mix together turkey, breadcrumbs, onion, garlic, basil, egg, red pepper flakes, soy sauce, salt, and pepper. Shape into balls about 1 inch in diameter.

4. Heat oil over medium-high heat, then add meatballs (in batches if necessary), turning two or three times during cooking time, until browned but not cooked through, about 5-7 minutes.

5. Place meatballs in a single layer in a 13 x 9-inch pan. Brush with half of hoisin sauce.

6. Bake until meatballs are cooked through, about 10-15 minutes. Remove from oven and let cool slightly.

7. Wrap each meatball with a ribbon of vegetable; secure with a wooden toothpick. Place on fresh, ungreased baking sheet; brush with remaining hoisin sauce. Bake for 10 minutes more.

BACON-WRAPPED MEATBALLS with LOADED SOUR CREAM

● ● ●

Warning: these guilty-pleasure meatballs might be the only thing you'll ever want to eat again! If it wasn't enough that they're wrapped in bacon, the accompanying dip contains an addictive "spice"–crunched-up Cool Ranch-flavored Doritos. For a little less guilt, substitute some or all of the sour cream with Greek yogurt.

LOADED SOUR CREAM

10–12 Cool Ranch-flavored Doritos
1 (16 ounce) carton sour cream
1 scallion, finely chopped
1 teaspoon apple cider vinegar
1 teaspoon hot sauce
1 teaspoon seasoned salt
½ teaspoon black pepper

BACON-WRAPPED MEATBALLS

1 large white potato, peeled and baked or boiled
1 pound ground beef
½ pound sweet pork sausage, bulk, or link with casings removed
½ pound hot pork sausage, bulk, or link with casings removed
1 medium onion, finely chopped
2 large eggs, lightly beaten
¼ cup milk
¼ cup Cheddar cheese, shredded
1 tablespoon Worcestershire sauce
1 teaspoon Dijon mustard
½ cup Italian breadcrumbs
1 teaspoon salt
1 teaspoon black pepper
1 cup barbecue sauce (from jar or the recipe on page 27)
2 pounds thick-cut bacon

1. Crunch Doritos into crumbs with a mortar and pestle or rolling pin. Combine with sour cream, scallion, apple cider vinegar, hot sauce, seasoned salt, and pepper. Cover and refrigerate for at least 1 hour.

2. Preheat oven to 350°F.

3. Mash potato with potato masher, then loosely mix with beef, sweet sausage, hot sausage, onion, eggs, milk, Cheddar cheese, Worcestershire sauce, mustard, breadcrumbs, salt, and pepper. Shape into balls about 1½ inches in diameter.

4. Wrap each meatball in a slice of bacon, secure with a toothpick, and place on raised wire rack or cookie sheet (if available) on top of baking sheet.

5. Bake for 20 minutes, then remove from oven and drain fat from pan. Brush with barbecue sauce. Bake until meatballs are cooked through and bacon is just starting to get crispy, about 15 minutes more, draining fat one more time through cooking time if necessary. Drain on paper towels if wire rack wasn't used. Serve with Loaded Sour Cream.

MOZZARELLA-STUFFED MEATBALLS

●●●

What's better than a meatball? A meatball with a ball of cheese inside! Buy fresh mozzarella cheese to make these meatballs over-the-top melty and delicious. If you can't find the small balls of mozzarella (often sold in 8-ounce plastic containers), buy bulk fresh mozzarella and cut it into ¾-inch cubes.

1 pound ground beef
1 pound ground veal
1 medium onion, finely chopped
3 garlic cloves, minced
2 slices white bread, crusts trimmed,
   torn into small pieces
¼ cup prepared Italian salad dressing
1 large egg, lightly beaten
3 tablespoons fresh parsley, chopped
1 teaspoon salt
½ teaspoon black pepper
6 ounces fresh mozzarella cheese balls
1 tablespoon vegetable or olive oil

1. Preheat oven to 450°F.

2. Loosely mix together beef, veal, onion, garlic, bread, Italian salad dressing, egg, parsley, salt, and pepper. Shape into balls about 1½-2 inches in diameter. Make well in each ball and fill with mozzarella cheese ball, then cover with meat to seal.

3. Heat oil in skillet over medium-high heat, then add meatballs (in batches if necessary), turning two or three times during cooking time, until browned but not cooked through, about 6-8 minutes.

4. Remove meatballs to baking sheet and place in oven. Bake until meatballs are cooked through, about 12-15 minutes.

MIX 'N' MATCH

Use Mozzarella-Stuffed Meatballs to make dishes like the Classic Italian Meatballs on page 80 more fun! They also go great on sandwiches, like in the Italian Meatball Subs on page 69.

OLIVE-STUFFED MEATBALLS

● ● ●

These delightful meatballs are sometimes called "Mexican surprise" meatballs because they have a tasty secret inside: a pimento-stuffed olive. They're great served over rice, or even as a nachos topping!

> 2 pounds ground beef
> 2 large eggs, lightly beaten
> 1 medium onion, finely chopped
> ¼ cup breadcrumbs
> ½ cup enchilada sauce or salsa
> 2 garlic cloves, minced
> 1 teaspoon salt
> ½ teaspoon black pepper
> 1 (12 ounce) jar pimento-stuffed olives
> 1 tablespoon vegetable or olive oil

1. Preheat oven to 350°F.

2. Loosely mix together beef, eggs, onion, breadcrumbs, enchilada sauce or salsa, garlic, salt, and pepper. Wrap each olive with meat mixture, forming meatballs about 1 inch in diameter.

3. Heat oil over medium-high heat, then add meatballs (in batches if necessary), turning two or three times during cooking time, until browned but not cooked through, about 5-7 minutes.

4. Place meatballs in a single layer in a 13 x 9-inch pan. Bake until meatballs are cooked through, about 15-20 minutes.

MIX 'N' MATCH

Try Olive-Stuffed Meatballs with the Mushroom Sauce on page 116!

SCOTCH EGGS

●●●

A scotch egg is a hard-boiled egg wrapped in sausage meat, and it tastes as delicious as it sounds. A common picnic food in the United Kingdom, they're often sold in British supermarkets, corner stores, and even gas stations. Stateside, you can find them in English pubs and at state fairs, sometimes on the end of a stick! They couldn't be simpler, so use high-quality eggs and sausage (if you can) to make them as rich with flavor as possible.

1 pound sausage with herbs, bulk,
   or link with casings removed
1 teaspoon Worcestershire sauce
1/8 teaspoon cayenne pepper
1/2 teaspoon salt
1/4 teaspoon black pepper
5 large eggs, hard-boiled and peeled
3/4 cup all-purpose flour
1 large egg, beaten
1 cup Italian breadcrumbs
Oil for frying

1. Loosely mix together sausage, Worcestershire sauce, cayenne pepper, salt, and pepper. Shape into five balls of equal size, then flatten.

2. Dust each hard-boiled egg lightly with flour, then wrap each flattened meatball around each egg, fully enclosing it.

3. Dip each meat-wrapped egg in flour again, then raw egg, then breadcrumbs.

4. Heat oil in deep-fryer or in a large pot (about 3 inches deep) on the stovetop to 350°F. Fry Scotch eggs in batches, turning during cooking time, until golden brown, about 10 minutes. Let drain on paper towels.

MIX 'N' MATCH

Scotch eggs are great with any kind of dipping sauce, like the Buffalo Sauce on page 102 and the Cuban Black Bean Sauce on page 124.

MY MEATBALL RECIPES

House Recipe #1

INGREDIENTS

_____
_____
_____
_____
_____
_____
_____
_____
_____
_____

1. _____
_____
_____

2. _____
_____
_____

3. _____
_____
_____

4. _____
_____
_____

5. _____
_____
_____

6. _____
_____

7. _____
_____

House Recipe #2

INGREDIENTS

_____
_____
_____
_____
_____
_____
_____
_____
_____
_____
_____

1. _____
_____

2. _____
_____

3. _____
_____

4. _____
_____

5. _____
_____

6. _____
_____

7. _____
_____

METRIC CONVERSIONS

OVEN TEMPERATURES

FAHRENHEIT	CELSIUS	BRITISH GAS MARK
250°F	120°C	N/A
275°F	140°C	1
300°F	150°C	2
325°F	170°C	3
350°F	180°C	4
375°F	190°C	5
400°F	200°C	6
425°F	220°C	7
450°F	230°C	8
475°F	240°C	9
500°F	260°C	N/A

VOLUME

US	METRIC
1/8 teaspoon	.5 milliliters
¼ teaspoon	1 milliliters
½ teaspoon	2 milliliters
¾ teaspoon	4 milliliters
1 teaspoon	5 milliliters
1 tablespoon	15 milliliters
¼ cup	60 milliliters
1/3 cup	80 milliliters
½ cup	120 milliliters
2/3 cup	160 milliliters
¾ cup	180 milliliters
1 cup	225 milliliters (dry), 250 milliliters (liquid)
2 cups (1 pint)	450 milliliters, 500 milliliters (liquid)
4 cups (1 quart)	1 liter
½ gallon	2 liters
1 gallon	4 liters

LENGTH

US	METRIC
¼ inch	6 millimeters
½ inch	13 millimeters
¾ inch	19 millimeters
1 inch	2½ centimeters
1 ½ inches	3¾ centimeters
2 inches	5 centimeters
2 ½ inches	6½ centimeters

WEIGHT

US	METRIC
1 ounce	28 grams
4 ounces (¼ pound)	113 grams
8 ounces (½ pound)	230 grams
12 ounces (¾ pound)	340 grams
16 ounces (1 pound)	450 grams
23 ounces (2 pounds)	900 grams

CONVERSIONS FOR COMMON INGREDIENTS

Breadcrumbs	
VOLUME	WEIGHT
2 tablespoons	20 grams
½ cup	100 grams
1 cup	150 grams

Cheese, shredded	
VOLUME	WEIGHT
2 tablespoons	11 grams
½ cup	60 grams
1 cup	90 grams

Flour, all-purpose	
VOLUME	WEIGHT
2 tablespoons	13 grams
½ cup	70 grams
1 cup	110 grams

Herbs, chopped	
VOLUME	WEIGHT
2 tablespoons	5 grams
½ cup	15 grams
1 cup	25 grams

Nuts, chopped	
VOLUME	WEIGHT
2 tablespoons	20 grams
½ cup	100 grams
1 cup	150 grams

Oats, uncooked	
VOLUME	WEIGHT
2 tablespoons	11 grams
½ cup	60 grams
1 cup	90 grams

Salt	
VOLUME	WEIGHT
2 tablespoons	40 grams
½ cup	200 grams
1 cup	300 grams

INDEX

Bold type indicates a page containing a recipe for that entry.